Penguin Education

Penguin Science of [illegible]
General Editor: B. M. F[illegible]

Social Psychology
Editor: Michael Argyle

Interpersonal Perception
Mark Cook

Interpersonal Perception

Mark Cook

Penguin Books

Penguin Books Ltd, Harmondsworth,
Middlesex, England
Penguin Books Inc., 7110 Ambassador Road,
Baltimore, Md 21207, U.S.A.
Penguin Books Australia Ltd,
Ringwood, Victoria, Australia

First published 1971
Copyright © Mark Cook, 1971

Made and printed in Great Britain by
Cox & Wyman Ltd, London, Reading and Fakenham
Set in Intertype Times

Penguin Science of Behaviour

This book is one in an ambitious project, the Penguin Science of Behaviour, which covers a very wide range of psychological inquiry. Many of the short 'unit' texts are on central teaching topics, while others deal with present theoretical and empirical work which the Editors consider to be important new contributions to psychology. We have kept in mind both the teaching divisions of psychology and also the needs of the psychologist at work. For readers working with children, for example, some of the units in the field of Developmental Psychology deal with psychological techniques in testing children, other units deal with work on cognitive growth. For academic psychologists, there are units in well-established areas such as Cognitive Psychology but also units which do not fall neatly under any one heading, or which are thought of as 'applied', but which nevertheless are highly relevant to psychology as a whole.

The project is published in short units for two main reasons. Firstly, a large range of short texts at inexpensive prices gives the teacher a flexibility in planning his course and recommending texts for it. Secondly, the pace at which important new work is published requires the project to be adaptable. Our plan allows a unit to be revised or a fresh unit to be added with maximum speed and minimal cost to the reader.

Above all, for students, the different viewpoints of many authors, sometimes overlapping, sometimes in contradiction, and the range of topics Editors have selected, will reveal the complexity and diversity which exists beyond the necessarily conventional headings of an introductory course.

B.M.F.

Contents

Editorial Foreword

This volume is in the social psychology section of the Science of Behaviour series. In this part of the series a number of volumes are planned which will give a comprehensive coverage of social psychology, each written by active research workers, and providing an up-to-date and rigorous account of different parts of the subject. There has been an explosive growth of research in social psychology in recent years, and the subject has broken out of its early preoccupation with the laboratory to study social behaviour in a variety of social settings. These volumes will differ somewhat from most existing textbooks: in addition to citing laboratory experiments they will cite field studies, and deal with the details and complexities of the phenomena as they occur in the outside world. Links will be established with other disciplines such as sociology, anthropology, animal behaviour, linguistics, and other branches of psychology, where relevant. As well as being useful to students, these monographs should therefore be of interest to a wide public – those concerned with the various fields dealt with.

Person perception, the subject of this book, is one of the central topics in social psychology, and one that is crucial to the understanding of social behaviour. It is also of practical importance in connection with the assessment of others for clinical purposes, in personnel selection, and in everyday life. Mark Cook has carried out a great deal of experimental research into person perception and related aspects of social interaction. In *Interpersonal Perception* he has produced a lively and critical account of a large and complex field of research. He places a certain amount of emphasis on the question of how accurate judgements of others are, and the conditions for greatest accuracy – topics which have been neglected in recent accounts of person perception. And he treats person perception as something that happens during ongoing social interaction, rather than as a kind of laboratory task, as it has sometimes been regarded.

M.A.

Preface

This book is intended as a short introduction to that area of social psychology variously called interpersonal perception, person perception and impression formation. These names give some indication of the content. It is a large area and the first chapter attempts to define its scope in greater detail.

Because this area is so large and the literature so extensive, and because this book is only a short introduction, many areas can only be discussed very briefly and some not at all. This means inevitably that many interesting studies are not referred to. Some omissions are accidental, but some are deliberate and the result of our approach to the area. We shall emphasize behavioural aspects of interpersonal perception and also the forming of judgements or impressions in actual encounters, but shall pay less attention to verbal report methods and even less to verbal presentation. This means that some large areas of research, notably studies using the semantic differential and lists of adjectives as stimulus material, will not be described in much detail. Some of the objections to such methods are set out in chapters 3 and 9. A second good reason for devoting less space to these studies is the existence of a recent, comprehensive review by Warr and Knapper (1968).

The size of the literature also creates a problem with references. It is undesirable in a book of this size to give 'chapter and verse' for every finding mentioned. Therefore, where literature reviews exist, they have been cited, and further details of the research mentioned can be obtained from them.

A final point needs to be made. Social psychology, like most areas of psychology, has not reached the stage where we can make very many unqualified assertions. On the other hand, continual qualifications of every statement make tedious reading, so we have stated what appear to be reasonable conclusions, without qualification. Some are no doubt questionable, but not, we hope, absurd.

I would like to thank all my colleagues and students for their contributions of ideas and references on the subject of person perception. I would like to thank Michael Argyle for his helpful comments on the manuscript, and his valuable advice on the book generally, and Robert McHenry for his illuminating thoughts on the subject of measuring accuracy of perception.

I would also like to thank my wife for her tolerance and understanding while I have been occupied writing this book.

M.C.

1 Introduction

Most people take the perception of others for granted and rarely stop to consider what opinions they form of others, why and how they form them and whether they are right. They select their friends without realizing why, trust some people and distrust others often for quite irrational reasons; they ask one girl for a date and not another without being able to say why, and possibly even get married without ever considering what their spouse is really like and whether they will be compatible. Yet if people are often unaware that they have formed opinions of others, in many cases the exact opposite happens; they form opinions about other people and assert them dogmatically, allowing them to affect their whole behaviour towards that person. How often do people form 'an instant dislike' of another person in a way that baffles everyone else, or insist, in the face of all the evidence, that someone is mean or unintelligent or the like?

Everyday 'informal' judgements of others can have far-reaching effects such as marriage; the same is even more true of 'professional' judgements. People are selected for jobs or higher education, etc., often on the basis of an interview in which the interviewer forms, on the basis of a fifteen-minute encounter, an opinion of the person's suitability, and, in the process, affects that person's life for years to come. Interviewers often never consider whether they are right or not, but rather have a firm belief in their own infallibility. Is this justified? If not, does it not follow that the interview should be abandoned as a form of assessment? The interview is the most important single type of 'professional' perception of others, but there are many more. Psychiatrists decide what is wrong with patients, and have complete confidence in the correctness of the (often highly unlikely) conclusions they draw. Social workers do the same for their 'clients'. School teachers give assessments of their pupils' ability and often of their behaviour, with complete confidence in their own judgement. The police and the courts decide whether someone has committed an offence or whether witnesses are telling the truth, and are generally confident that their verdicts are correct. Suppose that school teachers, lawyers, social workers are not correct in their opinions of others; it follows that they should either try to improve the quality of their assessments or stop making them, which would require a radical reform of education, social work, the law and many other institutions that depend on reliable judgements of people being made.

Few people consider that they are making judgements about others, and fewer still realize that they may be wrong about others much of the time. However the forming of opinions or impressions about others is one of the major topics of social psychology, and is called 'interpersonal perception' to distinguish it from the perception of material objects.

Interpersonal perception can be defined as the forming of judgements by people about other people, and more especially those judgements (which are the great majority) that concern people as social animals. Interpersonal perception does not concern itself with judgements about anatomy, physical dimension, height, etc., nor with reaction times or physiological responses unless these are visible, for example, blushing. However the word 'judgement' has misleading overtones. It implies both a concern only with conclusions reached after careful and judicious weighing of the evidence, and also that the person is aware of making a judgement and aware what the judgement is. In fact, very often the judge is not aware of making a judgement, and many judgements are made in a very haphazard fashion. A more precise description of the field of interpersonal perception might, therefore, be 'the study of the ways people react and respond to others, in thought, feeling and action'. For convenience throughout the book, the terms 'judge' and 'subject' will be used. 'Judge' refers to the person making the judgement (or reacting to another person); 'subject' refers to the person being judged (or reacted to). 'Subject' is also used to refer to anyone taking part in an experiment. It might help to consider some typical instances of interpersonal perception.

1. Candidates for a university, all with equally good qualifications, come for an interview after which some are given places and some are not.

2. A psychiatrist interviews a patient and eventually decides the patient should be classified as a 'hebephrenic schizophrenic'.

3. A man meets a girl, goes out with her for a while and decides that she is 'not his type'.

4. An office employee sees his employer coming in and decides that he is not 'in a good mood'.

5. A teacher in a class explains something to one of the pupils but realizes that the pupil has not understood.

6. During a conversation one person persistently but unintentionally interrupts the other because he fails to perceive that the other has not finished speaking.

It will be evident by now that interpersonal perception can cover a variety of judgements, decisions or reactions, on a number of different levels.

In this chapter the various types of judgements will be listed and classified; the second half of the chapter will be concerned with outlining the questions that can be asked about such judgements and giving a brief summary of the rest of the book.

Types of judgement

There is no systematic research on the content of judgements that people make about others, so the analysis in this section will be *a priori* and possibly inaccurate, suggesting people make judgements they do not in fact make, and omitting important judgements that are made frequently. The lack of research is curious; it would be easy to study the content of some types of judgements at least by questionnaire and survey methods; other types of judgements that the judge is not aware of making would present problems. Before listing and classifying judgements, an important distinction should be made. Some judgements concern enduring unchanging aspects of the person who is being judged. The first three judgements listed above fall into this type. The potential student's suitability for a university place is assumed to be a more or less fixed and static aspect of him. The psychiatrist's patient will continue to exhibit schizophrenic symptoms for some time, possibly indefinitely. The man who decides his potential girlfriend's personality is incompatible with his own does not expect that she will change. (Indeed, personality is sometimes defined as the enduring patterns of consistency in a person's behaviour.) Many attributes of people, such as personality, sex, age, intelligence, social class, sporting ability, etc., do not change very much from day to day. Some change gradually, like age and intelligence. Some change suddenly, but do not do so very often: for example, personality can be drastically altered by certain brain injuries, and social class can change abruptly if the person suddenly acquires a fortune, but these are rare events. Some aspects can change in one direction, but cannot be reversed; this applies particularly to learned abilities, for example, speaking a foreign language. Some aspects, like sex, are unchanging.

Other judgements, however, concern aspects of other people that change quite readily, over a period of days, hours or even seconds. In example 4 the employer's mood will probably last only a few hours. The pupil in example 5 obviously did not fail to understand the puzzling matter before the teacher explained it, and will probably not continue to fail to understand for longer than it takes the teacher to explain it again. In either case the employer's mood or the pupil's incomprehension are not permanent features of them. In example 6 the person who interrupts is probably failing to make a judgement about the other – that he has not finished speaking – where variations in the other's intentions occur almost from second to second.

Argyle (1969) distinguishes 'static' and 'dynamic' judgements; although the terms are not ideal, they will suffice. Static judgements are those that refer to enduring aspects of the other person, while dynamic judgements are concerned with aspects that change more rapidly. In fact 'static–dynamic' refers to a dimension rather than a dichotomy. Very few static judgements refer to aspects of people that never change: even sex can be surgically altered. The time scale of dynamic judgements can vary considerably. Moods, for example, may last for weeks, or only for an hour: they do not usually change from minute to minute, however. Other dynamic judgements necessarily concern things that alter very rapidly, as with the perception of whether someone has finished speaking or not. However, while the static–dynamic distinction is a dimension in terms of real time scales, it is a dichotomy for the perceiver. Certain things, like sex, personality, class, etc., are thought of as unchanging; people are often surprised when they find that someone has aged visibily or changed his job. On the other hand, people expect moods, intentions, etc., to change from time to time and so are not surprised if they do not remain constant.

Judgements of enduring characteristics (static judgements)

Superficial. A lot of judgements made about others concern relatively superficial characteristics: nationality, race, social class, occupation, age, physical appearance. This type of judgement is not particularly important in itself. However, these superficial characteristics often determine the initial impression a person makes, and elicit 'stereotypes' in the perceiver. Once a person has been perceived as old, or Irish or as being a doctor, a great number of characteristics tend to be attributed to him, some correctly, some incorrectly. P. E. Vernon (1964) points out that stereotypes based on perception of superficial characteristics are often very useful, since they enable the perceiver to select correct initial responses towards the other. It is also worth noting that judgements of superficial characteristics are mostly very easily verified.

Habitual responses to particular situations. This covers a great variety of judgements, of a type commonly made. Here are some examples:

He always slams the door
He drives too fast
She always dresses very smartly
He loses his way very easily
He plays football well
He votes Conservative
He doesn't believe in giving money to charity

The first three judgements concern the subject's usual response to a particular situation – what he does in given circumstances. The next two concern his abilities to do (relatively specific) things. The last two concern particular attitudes and beliefs the person holds. These judgements concern the subject's usual response and are 'dispositional' statements, like the sort that have been discussed by Ryle (1949). Ryle points out that such statements summarize previous behaviour and predict future behaviour.

Many judgements of this type go beyond description and explain why the person behaves that way:

He drives very fast because he is aggressive
He plays football well because he has fast reflexes
He doesn't believe in giving money to charity because he is mean

Judgements of habitual response to particular situations can be verified fairly easily; the explanations given for the behaviour are usually more difficult to verify.

Habitual responses to classes of situations. This is also a very large and important class of judgement. Here are some examples:

He is ill-mannered/salacious/sadistic.
He is mean/fatherly/submissive/rigid/tolerant
He is extraverted/anxious/intelligent.

Judgements of this type do not concern particular responses, but offer a general description of whole areas of behaviour. Characteristics like 'meanness' and 'extraversion' are called 'traits'. Some traits cover only a limited area of behaviour, for example, 'fatherliness', whereas others cover the whole of a person's behaviour, for example, 'extraversion'. There are many trait words in the English language; Allport and Odbert (1936) counted eighteen thousand.

Many interpersonal perception experiments have used personality traits that have been devised by psychologists and are not in common everyday use, for example:

He has a high need for achievement
He has an anal personality
He is very schizothymic

Judgement of response to classes of situations may also offer interpretation of the behaviour, for example:

He is ill-mannered because he doesn't like people
He is ill-mannered because he has been brought up badly
He is ill-mannered because he is basically insecure and trying to boost his self-confidence

'Trait' statements, like judgements of habitual responses to particular situations, summarize previous behaviour and predict future behaviour. They also are useful in communicating information about people. It is quicker to say that someone is extraverted than to describe all the relevant behaviour. The communication is liable to be imprecise however, since different receivers may interpret the label 'extraverted' in terms of different sets of behaviour.

'Trait' statements are particularly hard to verify, since they do not entail any particular set of behaviours. An extraverted person may show any one of a very large set of items of extraverted behaviour, so the absence of any particular item does not conclusively disprove the statement. This poses problems when we attempt to determine the accuracy of a trait statement.

Sociometric judgements. The types of judgements discussed so far concern one person's behaviour, attitudes, abilities. It is possible to make such judgements about that person without considering any other person. Sociometric judgements concern relations between people and so involve two or more persons. (In many such judgements the judge himself is involved in the comparison.)

Examples of sociometric judgements are:

Jones does not like me
Jones does not like Smith
Jones is afraid of me
Jones dominates/has influence over Smith

Most of the research to be reported has restricted itself to relations of like and dislike; we should note however that relations between people can be more subtle than simple like–dislike and dominance–submission. We speak of a great variety of relations between people: fear, hate, contempt, worship, envy, love, pity, etc.

So far we have been talking about the simple perception of relations between people; it is possible to study more complicated relationships, such as:

Jones perceives that Smith knows Jones does not like him
Jones perceives that Smith knows that Brown does not like Jones
Jones perceives that Smith knows that Brown does not like Smith

Judgements like these may seem very obscure and unlikely when written down, but in fact such judgements are often made and are often of great importance.

It is often important to perceive the opinions of a group rather than of a single person; for example, a lecturer or public speaker perceives the mood of his audience – attentive or bored, sympathetic or hostile, etc. Politicians and journalists try to judge the opinion of whole communities. It can be argued that such judgements involve no more than forming a number of judgements about individuals; this may be true, but since it has been shown that judgements of group opinion and individual opinion are separate skills (see chapter 7) they will be regarded as separate types of judgement.

In most cases judgements will be formed on the basis of personal contact and will be about people the judge interacts with; some judgements may be formed at a distance, however, and will concern people the judge does not meet. People form impressions of politicians and other public figures, both of their personal characteristics and of their attitudes and intentions; people also form opinions about groups of people they have never met. The information on which these judgements are based comes mainly through the mass media.

Judgements of changing characteristics (dynamic judgements)

It has already been pointed out that it may be false to dichotomize static and dynamic judgements, since we are dealing with a dimension of time over which various features change. Certainly some of the dynamic judgements concern aspects of the other person that have already been considered, as enduring characteristics.

Specific responses. Previously we discussed habitual responses to particular situations; now we are considering responses on a particular occasion, for example:

He will want to go to the cinema this evening
He has damaged my car
He will not be able to solve this problem
He has not won his tennis match
He has voted Conservative today
He will refuse to sign this petition

Some judgements of this type are predictive, whereas others are retrospective.

[In the retrospective (second, fourth and fifth) examples, we are assuming the judgement is not based on direct evidence, that is, we do not know he has damaged the car, because he says so, or we saw it; rather we have inferred from more indirect evidence.]

Judgements of this type may include interpretation of the behaviour, for example:

He wants to leave now because he is bored
He cannot answer my question because he wasn't listening
He is going to vote Conservative because of their foreign policy

Judgements of this type are very similar to judgements of the next type, and to some extent the distinction is arbitrary.

Affective judgements. There are three types of affective judgement. The first type is the judgement of moods, emotions and similar states of individuals. These are almost as numerous and varied as trait judgements. Below is a list of some of the states a person may be said to be in:

surprise
fear
suffering
anger
determination
disgust
contempt
love
happiness
mirth
irritation
impatience
fatigue
intoxication

Sometimes we limit the judgement to the simple observation that the person is angry, impatient, etc. More usually, however, the judgement also involves the target or cause of the state, for example:

He is angry with me
He is angry with Jones
He is angry with Jones because Jones contradicted him

The second class of affective judgements concerns the subject's reaction to what someone (possibly the judge himself) has said, for example:

He does not agree with that
He does not understand that
He does not believe that
He is not listening to what I am saying

The third class of affective judgement concerns the speaker's attitude to what he says. People do not always stand in the same relation to the things they say; for example, the speaker's manner can indicate that he really means the opposite of what he said. Below is a list of six variations in the speaker's attitude to what he is saying, taken from Liberman (1965):

a bored statement
a confidential communication
expressing disbelief or doubt
an objective question
an objective statement
a pompous statement

(Some of these variations in attitude are not deliberate.)

Regulation. It has recently been pointed out that encounters require 'regulation' or 'management'. Besides forming opinions about the person it is necessary to respond correctly to certain other information he gives, concerning the interaction itself. For example, it is necessary to ensure that no more than one person talks at a time and, in many situations, that at least one person talks, that is, there are no silences;

some recent work has studied the signals by which this regulation occurs. It is also necessary to decide when the interaction itself should start and finish, and possibly when it should progress from one stage to another. Thirdly, the emotional tone of the encounter must be controlled, an 'equilibrium' maintained. For example, responses that are appropriate in a family argument are quite wrong in a casual conversation or a business encounter, and would alter the emotional tone. The people in an encounter decide what sort of encounter it is and so refrain from inappropriate behaviour that would alter the nature of the encounter.

Summary of the layout of the book

In this section, we will consider what questions may usefully be asked about interpersonal perception and, in doing so, indicate the order and contents of the remaining chapters.

Processes involved in forming judgements

The most important problems for the psychologist are how judgements of others are formed, what the successive stages involved are and what factors need to be taken into consideration. In chapter 2, two different types of explanation of the judgement process are considered. Because the judgements we can make about other people are very diverse, it is possible that different models will be required for different types of judgement. In chapter 2, we will also consider whether the same model will account for judgements of static characteristics and for judgements of changing characteristics during an ongoing encounter. We will also consider whether the model for describing interpersonal perception bears any relationship to the models put forward for describing the perception of objects.

General ideas about other people

Our consideration of the processes involved in interpersonal perception, in chapter 2, will lead us to the conclusion that a very important part of the judgement process are the general propositions that we hold about other people. These will be considered in chapters 3 and 4. In chapter 3 we will consider ideas about the association of characteristics and see what sort of attributes are thought to be associated, how these tend to form large groups in most individual conceptual systems and how often they are incorrect or systematically biased. In chapter 4 we will consider a different class of ideas about others – those concerned with the distinguishing characteristics, in behaviour and appearance, of people who are thought to have particular attributes.

Accuracy

When we form an opinion about someone, it usually affects our subsequent behaviour towards that person. If we decide that someone is not intelligent, we do not entrust them with difficult and complex tasks. If we decide someone is not honest, we do not allow them to handle our money. If we decide someone is prone to anxiety, we avoid exposing them to stressful situations. Since judgements about people affect our behaviour towards them, it is important that they should be accurate. If we decide that someone is intelligent when he is not, or that he does not like us when he does, the consequences could be unfortunate. One of the principal areas of study has, therefore, been the accuracy of our perception of others. Chapter 6 describes the work that has been done on the accuracy with which judgements of different types are made. However, the measurement of accuracy of perception involves a number of methodological artefacts which have beset studies in this area and made many of them hard to interpret. These difficulties are discussed in chapter 5 which is more technical than the rest of the book. Some conclusions do emerge, however, and the occurrence of the artefacts themselves throws some light on interpersonal perception.

The generality of ability to judge others

We sometimes describe people as 'very perceptive' or 'very sharp' or as 'a good judge of people'. We imply by this that the person makes accurate judgements about other people and that all his judgements, whatever their content, are equally accurate. We make a great variety of judgements so it is relevant to ask whether accuracy of judgement is general across all judgement tasks, or whether it is specific to particular types of judgements. For example, is a person who is good at judging intelligence also good at judging who likes who in a group, or what mood someone is in? It has been suggested that the ability to judge others is general, like intelligence itself, or it may be specific to different situations.

When we talk about someone being a good judge of others, we tend to attribute to him other characteristics, for example, stability, social poise and possibly intelligence. It seems at any rate a plausible assumption that a good judge of others will be a different sort of person from a very bad judge of others. (This assumes of course that the ability to judge is general.) The literature on generality of ability to judge and on characteristics of good judges is discussed in chapter 7.

Practical applications

Judgements of others are made in everyday life and in the laboratory; many judgements, often of a specialized type, are made professionally. For example, selection of candidates for jobs or university involves forming a judgement of that person, by one or more judges. Chapter 8 discusses some instances of specialized professional judgements and reviews their accuracy, the cues used in making them and ways of improving their accuracy where it is poor.

Summing up

The final chapter attempts to draw some conclusions from the work described in the preceding chapters, and suggests some directions for future research.

2 How we Form Judgements about Others

As we saw in chapter 1, we are constantly forming a wide variety of judgements about other people. The most important questions for the psychologist are how these judgements are formed, what processes are involved in interpersonal perception and how they were related. This chapter will be concerned with the various models that have been put forward to account for judgements of enduring and changing characteristics. Three questions will be considered.

The first has a long history of argument rather than an experiment. Is perception of others inferential or intuitive? In other words does the judge look at the other person and infer, from what he sees and hears, his opinion about him, or does he look and listen and then form a judgement immediately or 'intuitively'?

Secondly, there is the question whether the same model of perception can account for all types of judgement, or whether different models are required. Little attention seems to have been paid to this question; many models have been developed for static judgements and rather fewer for dynamic judgements, but no attempt has been made to integrate the two.

A final question is whether perception of people has anything in common with the perception of objects and, if not, what the differences are.

Both inference and intuition theories of perception, but more especially the latter, have been stated many times in different ways. In this section, therefore, the principal versions of each theory will be described, the relative merits of each discussed and the relevant empirical evidence described.

Intuition theories

An excellent review of intuition theories and a discussion of the concept of intuition is given by Sarbin, Taft and Bailey (1960). Intuition theorists in general do not state their theories very clearly and it is often difficult to determine exactly what they mean. In fact intuition theories put forward three different propositions.

1. Perception is innate. Thomas Reid (1764) said, 'Nature is so constituted that certain empirical facts are signs of certain metaphysical facts and human nature is so constituted as to be able to interpret these signs intuitively.' 'Natural signs' include facial expressions, gestures, etc. Reid is stating the proposition that the expression of certain states and their recognition are innate. Darwin (1872) also considered the expression and recognition of emotional states to be innate and to have evolved from adaptive responses to particular circumstances.

2. Perception is 'global'. The 'Verstehen' school of psychologists (Spranger, 1928) stated that people understand others by 'an act of intuition encompassing their personality as a whole'. Gestalt psychologists also emphasize the global aspect of perception by suggesting that people, like objects, are perceived as meaningful wholes.

3. Perception is 'immediate' or 'direct'. This proposition is the source of the obscurity in intuition theories. Austin (1962) points out that, in the context of perception, ' "directly" takes whatever sense it has from the contrast with its opposite'. Unless we are contrasting direct perception of people with some specified form of indirect perception – hearing evidence, seeing someone in a film – it is meaningless to talk of 'direct' perception. The suggestion that perception is direct or immediate sometimes implies that it is also infallible. As we shall see in chapters 3 and 4, this is far from true; our perceptions are often systematically biased and sometimes totally incorrect. The conviction that a belief or judgement is correct is no guarantee whatever that it is veridical. There are two theories that offer some explanation of

the distinction between direct and indirect: Gestalt theories and 'empathy' theories.

The Gestalt theory of person perception relies on the concept of 'isomorphism' and is presented by Arnheim (1949). The 'psychic structure' of the subject's mood is reflected in an isomorphic pattern of physiological forces, which in turn produce an isomorphic pattern of facial expression and posture. This is perceived by the observer and translated back into an isomorphic psychic structure in the observer, who thereby perceives the other's mood. This explanation is far from satisfactory. Indeed it is not an explanation at all. What is 'psychic structure' and how is it determined? In what sense can physiological forces be similar to facial expression and posture? And does not the theory imply that the observer will share the other's mood, rather than perceive it?

The 'empathy' theory states that the observer knows what the subject is feeling, because he imagines himself in similar circumstances and reacts accordingly. Direct perception in this version of the theory is being contrasted with indirect perception, in the sense that the observer is responding to the situation itself, rather than observing the subject. This is a valid hypothesis and one on which there is some evidence.

(We can offer a third explanation of the distinction between direct and indirect perception. It could be taken to mean that perception of emotions, or other states, is direct in that it does not require any identification or description of physical appearance of the subject. This point will be developed further later in the chapter.)

We should note that these three propositions in intuition theories are not logically related, although Gestalt theorists tend to assume they are related, as they do in other areas of perception. The question whether the ability to perceive others is inherited is quite separate from the question whether perception is global. The two may both be true, but it does not follow logically, so the relationship should be proved, not assumed. The relation between innateness of perception and its immediacy is a little more complicated. If perception is immediate, it must be innate, since it is hard to see how such immediate perceptions could be learned. However, the converse does not follow. It seems possible to conceive of perception as being innate and inferential; the ability to make certain types of inferences might be innate or learned.

Evidence for the propositions of intuition theories

Innateness. There is considerable evidence that expression of emotional states is to some extent innately determined in man and animals. Ekman (1969) shows that facial expression of simple emotional states is similar in a number of cultures, and further that children born blind show recognizable facial expressions. A later study (Ekman, Sorenson and Friesen, 1969) establishes that these facial expressions are recognized pan-culturally. There is an extensive literature on expression of emotion in a wide variety of species (see Vine, 1969, for a review); it has also been established (Sackett, 1965) that monkeys reared in isolation respond appropriately to facial expressions of other monkeys, thus showing that recognition can be innate.

While there is evidence that expression and recognition of emotion may be innate in man as well as animals, there is no evidence that other sorts of judgement depend on innate abilities. Indeed, it is obvious that the majority of them must be learned, for it is inconceivable that the ability to make judgements like those listed on page 18 – concerning responses to specific situations – could be innate.

Perception is global. There is ample evidence that impressions tend to be organized in meaningful ways, that people tend to assume associations between different characteristics and that discrepant information tends to be ignored or distorted. (This evidence is discussed in detail in chapter 3.) However, it is also obvious that people can give judgements on isolated aspects of personality, sometimes from isolated items of information. It follows that perception is not *necessarily* global – an act of understanding encompassing the person as a whole, as Spranger claims.

Perception is direct or immediate. We said before that this proposition has no meaning unless the nature of the contrast being made is stated. We have also said that the Gestalt concept of 'isomorphism' is unsatisfactory. The 'empathy' hypothesis is more satisfactory. Stotland (1969) defines empathy as experiencing an emotional reaction as a result of perceiving another experiencing an emotional reaction. As we said before it is direct in the sense that the empathizer reacts to the situation and feels the same way as the subject, rather than observing the subject's mood. Stotland produces evidence that empathy can occur, although he comments on a lack of consistency in the results. However, it is obvious that not all perception of emotion can depend on empathy, for people are quite able to judge another's mood or emotion without sharing it, that is, empathizing.

Stotland also points out that although studies of the perception of personality traits have been referred to as empathy studies, they do not involve empathy in this sense, for they involve prediction of another's response but not sharing of it. It seems doubtful whether empathy in the sense of sharing a response could apply except to emotional responses.

To conclude this section on intuition theories of interpersonal perception, we have seen that three unrelated claims are being made. These three claims all have some degree of truth, although two of them – that perception is direct and that it is innate – apply only to judgements of emotional states. The third – that perception is global – is true of many judgements, but is not a necessary feature of perception. We have also seen that the claim that perception is direct – the most important feature of intuition theories – is meaningless unless we can say what we mean by indirect perception.

Inference theory

The intuition theories are unsatisfactory because they do not explain how judgements are formed, for we have seen that the notion of direct or immediate perception is meaningless. The inference models do provide a satisfactory explanation of how judgements are made. They state quite simply that particular judgements are inferred from the evidence available and from general principles about human behaviour. The inferences can be considered as syllogisms (although it has been pointed out that the actual conceptual processes involved might not be strictly syllogistic in form). Here is an example:

All red-haired men are aggressive
This man has red hair
Therefore he is aggressive

The first proposition states a general principle about people. The second notes that the person under consideration has particular attributes and the third draws the inference that he has a further attribute. The general propositions are variously called 'postulates', 'schemata', 'constructs' and 'inference rules'. We will call them 'inference rules'.

We should note that the inference theory is not strictly speaking a theory, but an explanatory model using an analogy with symbolic logic. It gives us a useful framework for studying person perception but does not generate any testable predictions. We should also note that although the inferences made can be put in a syllogistic form, they are rarely strictly logical. Terms like 'all' and 'some' are used very loosely. The model also tends to emphasize the role of learning in acquiring ideas about others, although this is not an essential feature.

Objections to inference theory

The principal objection that can be made against the inference model relies on introspective evidence. When we form impressions and pass judgements of other people, we are not always aware of going through the quasi-syllogistic procedure described above. We do not approach social encounters as if we were a combination of a detective seeking clues and a logician drawing inferences. We 'just know' that the other person is angry or that he is aggressive. We cannot say what general principle and what items of evidence we used to reach the conclusion. This objection is easily dismissed. In the first place it is an appeal to introspection and, therefore, suspect; and, secondly, the process may occur without awareness. 'Unconscious inferences' have been convincingly demonstrated in other areas of perception. We infer that one object is further away than another because it seems smaller than the other, whereas we know from experience that they are actually the same size. We are not conscious of these inferences, but if the experimenter falsifies the premises – by constructing artificial objects of the wrong size – it is easy to show that such inferences are being made. (There are other cues to distance; see Gibson, 1950, for a discussion.)

It might be useful to distinguish a 'weak' form of the intuition hypothesis. We could take intuitive judgements to be those where the perceiver is not aware of making an inference, that is, he is not aware of the inference rule and the behavioural evidence that led him to form a judgement. Allport (1961) reports that people who adopt an analytic, reflective approach to perception are less accurate than those who adopt a more global, intuitive approach.

The real advantage of the inference model, however, is its fruitfulness; the intuition model does not give particularly illuminating answers to questions about person perception and has given rise to little or no research. The inference model, on the other hand, raises many interesting questions and gives a conceptual framework for a wide variety of empirical work.

Rule systems

Each person has a set of rules for classifying and responding to other people. Typical rules are: 'People who do not offer

cigarettes to others are mean' or 'People who lack perseverance will not succeed.' These systems of rules are one
of the more interesting areas of research in interpersonal perception, and there are a number of ways of studying them
and a number of aspects of them that may be studied. We
may distinguish two types of rule. Some state that particular
characteristics are associated, for example, 'People who lack
perseverance are unlikely to succeed' or 'People who are
intelligent are well adjusted.' The second type of rule gives
directions for identifying people who have a particular
characteristic, for example, 'People who do not offer their
cigarettes are mean' or 'People who interrupt one are rude.'
We will call the first type 'association rules' and the second
type 'identification rules'. Both have been studied extensively. The research of identification rules is described in
chapter 3, and that on association rules in chapter 4.

Figure 1 presents the inference model schematically. The
judge has information from three sources: the subject himself, the context and from memory and report. The judge
infers from an identification rule and from the information
he has that the subject belongs to a particular class of
persons. He may then go on to make further inferences using
associative rules. One such further inference is shown in the
model; in fact the judge might make several in a series.
People vary in the readiness with which they categorize
others; some reserve their judgement until they have plenty
of data, whereas others seem to have an almost obsessional
need to categorize everyone they meet as quickly as possible.

The nature of the inference itself depends on the circumstances of the judgement; even though the judge has a given
set of rules and the same information about the subject, it
does not follow he will make the same judgement every
time. In some circumstances, the judge may be interested in
moral aspects of the subject's behaviour, whereas in other
circumstances, he might be interested in more practical
aspects, for example, whether the subject can help him or
not. In more casual encounters, the judge will probably be

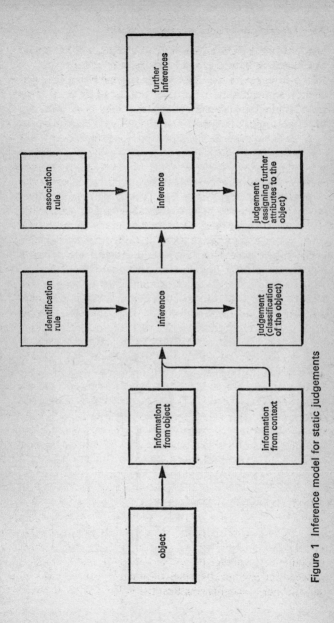

Figure 1 Inference model for static judgements

interested only in the role of the subject, rather than his 'deeper' personality.

The inference model has given rise to much research already and could inspire much more. It is also reasonably clear and logically sound; the intuition model, on the other hand, inspires little or no research, and is obscure and logically unsatisfactory. Evidently the inference model is preferable.

Models for static and dynamic judgements

The inference model was devised primarily for static judgements; for example, Sarbin, Taft and Bailey's version of the model was intended to explain clinical judgements. It is important to know whether these models can account for dynamic judgements. In this section a model for dynamic judgements will be discussed in relation to the inference model. This model is the social skill model of Argyle and Kendon (1967) and is illustrated in Figure 2.

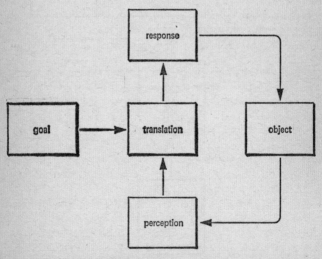

Figure 2 Simple social skill model

The social skill model is an analogy with motor skills and postulates four basic processes operating during interaction. The operator perceives the other person, decides what to do in order to achieve his goal, does it and then examines the result. For example, the operator's goal might be to borrow money. He sees that the subject is unwilling, because he fears he might not be repaid; in the operator's experience, the best response is to offer assurances and possibly security that the money will be repaid. He does this and observes continued reluctance and decides that the subject is now afraid of being left short of money; the operator now points out that he only wants to borrow a small sum. If he succeeds in borrowing the money the interaction will be terminated and a new goal pursued; if he does not, he may try another method, or give up, that is, change his goal.

The relevant part of the social skill model is 'perception', so our first step is to expand the perception phase of the model to include an inference process. This is illustrated in Figure 3. Various differences between the models now become apparent. Whereas the static inference model (Figure 1) stops once a judgement has been formed, the skill model continues to take account of the judge's response to the subject. In psychological experiments, judges commonly make judgements about subjects they see on film, and never actually meet, so the judgements have no actual consequence; in real life, judgements are made with some purpose, about people the judge knows and has dealings with. Frijda (1969) reports that his judges never described photos of emotional expressions in abstract terms, like those normally imposed on the subject in such experiments, but always in a way involving the subject, the judge himself and a concrete situation.

Secondly, perception is not usually a 'one off' process; judges do not usually make a single judgement and then stop, particularly with dynamic judgements. The initial perception and judgement leads to an initial response that has some effect on the subject, and this effect is in turn perceived and acted on, and so on. The process is continuous and circular, so long as the interaction continues. Indeed many responses are made specifically to produce a response in the other, that will provide further information about him; for example, questions are asked to clear up uncertain points, and situations created to evoke behaviour. Furthermore, perception and response tend to occur at the same time. One of the features of skilled performance is the development of overlapping perception and response; while the operator is responding to what he has just seen, he is already looking ahead to the next part of the task.

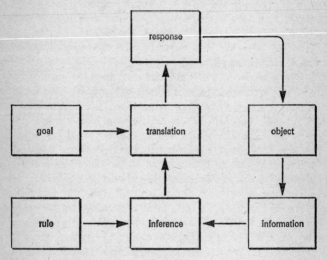

Figure 3 Expanded social skill model

There are many different types of judgement that can be made about others, on different levels of importance and extension in time. The model as specified so far can account for any judgement; however, we may ask whether people make more than one judgement at a time and, if so, whether the model should include more than one channel, operating in parallel. Argyle and Kendon suggest that there are two levels. On the first one, the judge makes judgements about the other's behaviour – these may or may not be conscious judgements. However, on the second level, he is also perceiving and responding to signals concerned with the 'maintenance' or 'regulation' of the interaction itself. During the interaction the subjects must ensure that they do not interrupt or leave silences, that they remain facing each other and that they look at appropriate moments and so forth. There is also evidence that gestures and facial movements are synchronized, although the purpose of this, if any, is not known. It is possible that this process of 'regulation' occurs in parallel with perception of the other's moods, intentions, etc., and does not use the same channel. However, the 'regulation' process operates in the same way as the other judgements. The judge observes that the other has ceased speaking and is looking up at him, so he infers that the other has finished his utterance, and himself starts speaking. The goal is usually constant – to maintain the interaction. Evidently the suggestion that there are two parallel channels, operating in continuous social encounters, is speculative and should be confirmed empirically; as elsewhere, methods might be borrowed from visual perception studies to test the hypothesis.

The completed model of interpersonal perception, presented in Figure 4, includes a few modifications. As Sarbin, Taft and Bailey point out, the goal of the encounter can affect the nature of the inferences made, as well as the response selected. The goal and the nature of the inference to be drawn can also affect the previous step in the process. If the judge wants to borrow money and is looking for signs of willingness, he may 'refer back' to the information he has for additional data. Also Argyle and Kendon point out that there is a third type of feedback; the interactor's goal itself may be changed by the other subject. For example, a person may set out to try to convert someone to vote Labour and instead himself be persuaded to vote Conservative.

The model originally proposed for static judgements has been considerably expanded and can now take account of a greater number of factors. The revised model may not be correct and some aspects – particularly the existence of the hypothesized second channel – need verification. In general however, the model offers a fuller and more satisfactory explanation than the intuition hypothesis, which at times seems to say only that perception is inexplicable.

Similarities and differences between perception of people and objects

Classic visual perception research has studied the perception of colour, brightness, shape, size and distance, and movement, but less attention has been paid to the recognition of familiar objects. M. D. Vernon (1952) reports a number of studies and Gregory (1966) outlines an interesting model for such recognition. Gregory suggests that people form 'hypotheses' about objects they see; if the object has certain attributes, then it is seen as a particular thing, whereas if it is ambiguous and could be one of two different things, like a Necker cube, it will alternate between the two possibilities. The attributes must be defined strictly enough to prevent frequent misidentifications, but also in a very elastic way to allow for the different appearances of the object from differing angles, under different levels of illumination, at different distances, etc. Some 'hypotheses' must also allow the perceiver to identify, as members of one class, objects that are not identical; for example, cars come in a variety of shapes, sizes, colours, etc., but are nevertheless recognized as cars. The process of identification is very rapid, except when the object is ambiguous. One study found that letters could be identified in as little as one-hundredth of a second, although later work suggests that exposure times as short as this cannot be taken at their face value, because of the operation of a short-term visual memory. One study found that identification of more complex and less easily discriminable shapes – aeroplane silhouettes – needed much longer, from one-tenth to one-fifth of a second. Even so, identification is very rapid and obviously could not depend on conscious reasoning processes.

It will be evident by now that the identification of objects and the perception of people have many similarities. Both involve the forming of inferences about the person or object,

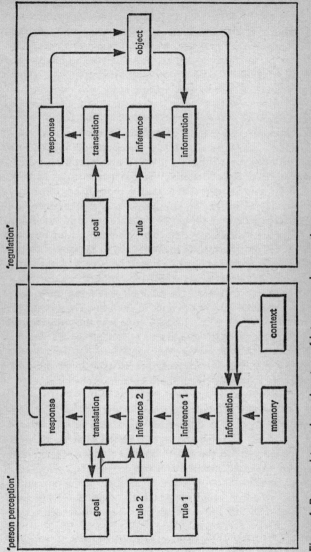

Figure 4 Proposed two-channel system of interpersonal perception

on the basis of what is seen and what was known before. In both the perceiver has a number of rules or generalizations or concepts that tell him what particular things or emotional states or personalities look like, and in both the inference from the data and the generalization or concept to the conclusion can be very rapid and unconscious.

'One stage further on'

It is commonly said that the perception of emotions, moods, personality, etc., differs from the perception of objects, in that it is 'one stage further on'. Thus, if an object fits a large and very elastic list of criteria, it is seen as a car; the identification of a facial expression, on the other hand, involves first the identification of physical characteristics, then a further inference from the emotional state of the person. But do we need to postulate a further inference? If an object fits one list of criteria it is identified as a car; why should there not be a similar list of criteria defining a particular emotion? One answer is that the criteria for identifying an angry face are of a different sort from those required for identifying a car and, in fact, involve the prior identification of physical objects. Let us take the criteria for an angry person as (for the sake of argument) 'red face and loud harsh voice'. However, the mention of 'red face' as a sign of anger is only a convenience of exposition; the requirements are really much more complex and might start 'an ellipse or comparable figure, of a particular size, in relation to distance and other surrounding shapes, etc.'. (It is in fact almost impossible to describe what is seen without using words that identify objects; after all that is what words are for.) Possibly those theorists who said that perception of emotions was direct meant that it was not one stage removed from judgements about physical appearance of the face and that the perceiver could recognize an 'angry face' just as readily and in just the same way as he would recognize a 'spotty face' or a 'red face'.

However, some judgements about people do take a long time to form and do involve the conscious weighing of evidence. Thus a psychoanalyst presumably takes some time and thought to decide that a person is 'fixated at the anal period' and does not recognize the state within one-tenth of a second. However, the same is true for some judgements of physical objects; experts will examine aerial photographs for some time before deciding what they represent.

The discussion so far has been speculative; however, the number of stages or processes involved in perceiving a particular type of material is an empirical question that should be settled by research. There are well-tried methods of deciding the question, mostly involving tachistoscopic exposures; if it takes longer to recognize an angry face than it does to recognize a red face, then there is probably another stage involved, and if it does not, there is probably no extra stage.

There is no fundamental difference between perception of people and of objects, but there are a number of reasons for supposing that there should be a difference. In the first place, people are more active than most objects, and cause more things to happen. They are for this reason more unpredictable than most objects. Also people have far more emotional significance than objects, so that judgements about them are more important and more emotionally loaded. Thirdly, people cannot be observed and discussed in the same way as objects, for they are also observing and so are conscious of any scrutiny and discussion. Finally, when we perceive another person, we have, or think we have, an extra source of information that we do not have when observing objects. We are observing another human being like ourselves, so we think we know more about the way he is behaving and thinking. However, none of these four differences represents a difference in kind.

To conclude this section, there is no sound reason for supposing that the perception of people and of objects differ in any important respect.

3 The General Principles about Others we Use to Form Judgements

Chapter 2 outlined a model of interpersonal perception according to which we infer a particular conclusion from general principles about others and from specific information. We referred to the general principles as inference rules and suggested that there were two types of inference rule: those stating that particular attributes were associated – association rules – and those that gave directions for recognizing people who possessed a particular attribute – identification rules. (Identification rules, in fact, tell us what the specific information needed in the second stage of the inference is.) In this chapter we will be considering primarily association rules, although much of what will be said will apply also to identification rules, particularly the sections on rigidity and on the origins of inference rules.

Methods of studying associative rule systems

There are four types of method used to study associative rules – free description, the Role Repertory Grid Test, the 'cue trait' method and the semantic differential.

Free description

This requires little comment. The judge is asked to describe a specified person in his own words; generally the result is then content analysed. This method has not been used very widely.

The Role Repertory Grid Test

This was devised by Kelly (1955). In the original form the subject is asked to consider twenty people, in groups of three at a time, and to say how two of them differ from the third,

After he has done this a number of times for different sets of three people, the resulting 'grid' is analysed to determine the number of 'constructs', or ways of classifying people, the person has, as well as their relative importance to him. The number of independent 'constructs' is often surprisingly small, for people tend to use the same classification very widely, but give it different names, so that everyone they class as 'likeable' is also classed as 'good looking', 'intelligent' and 'friendly'. Most 'grids' have a prominent evaluative construct, that accounts for much of the subject's classification of others. There are many different versions of the Repertory Grid Test and they are described by Bonarius (1965). These later versions of the test have tended to make it shorter and more artificial. The subject does not use his own words to describe his classifications, but makes use of 'provided constructs'. In some versions he does not judge real people he knows, but is provided with photographs of strangers.

The cue trait method

This was devised by Bruner, Shapiro and Tagiuri (1958) and has been used very widely since. It is very simple. The judge is told to think of an intelligent person and is then asked to say how likely he thinks it is that that person would be aggressive, sociable, selfish, etc. The results are analysed to discover which traits the subjects assumes to be correlated.

The semantic differential

The semantic differential was devised by Osgood, Suci and Tannenbaum (1957) but its origins may be traced back to Asch (1946). The judge gives his judgement on a series of bipolar scales, for example:

soft — — — — — — hard
warm — — — — — — cold
nice — — — — — — nasty

The ratings are scored from 1 to 7 (Asch required his subjects only to check one of the adjectives, giving binary data).

The data is then factor analysed, to determine which scales are correlated.

Research on association rules

There are a number of aspects of associative rule systems that may be studied: content, systematic biases, stability and rigidity, and origins. The study of these four aspects of associative rules systems has been one of the most fruitful areas of research in interpersonal perception carried out recently.

Content

The largest body of work has been done on the most obvious and important aspect of associative rule systems – their content. This can be further subdivided.

1. Some research has been reported on the component terms of association rules – as opposed to the rules themselves. Obviously it is useful to know what attributes are thought important in the first place, before we go on to consider how these attributes are related. (From a strictly logical point of view, this research should have been considered in chapter 1. However the research has been closely related to research on association rules themselves – both tending to use the repertory grid – so it will be reported here.)

Secord and Backman (1964) report some interesting data, using a free description method. They report that some subjects describe superficial aspects of others, like their appearance, whereas others go rather deeper and comment on the other person's motivations, conflicts, relations with people, etc. Little (1968a, 1968b) finds that women make more use of personality and interpersonal terms in describing others, whereas men describe others more in terms of role, achievement and physical characteristics. The attributes people mention also vary as a function of age, and the proportion of psychological terms used increases from the age of thirteen or fourteen. Adolescent girls tend to describe others in terms of their physical appearance to a great extent, forming an exception to the general rule that women talk less in physical terms and more in psychological terms. Crockett (1965) has summarized a number of studies using a free description measure of the number of concepts subjects use. A study of the number of concepts used to describe liked and disliked people of differing ages and different sex produced complex results, which tended to support the general principle that people have more concepts for dealing with those they interact with more frequently. Another study showed that subjects with many concepts for dealing with others were better able to integrate conflicting information about another person.

2. Having considered the sort of attributes people think relevant when describing others, and the number of different concepts they use, we can consider the relations people expect to find between different attributes – their association rules. Research in this area has shown that although people may use many different words to describe others, they do not use them independently. People expect one attribute to be associated with another. Often it is found that a number of apparently quite different attributes are associated for a particular judge. These groupings of attributes can be very broad, so that a dozen or more descriptive terms will all be used in the same way. Some recent research has tried to establish that everybody tends to use a small number of very broad classifications, while other research has looked at the difference between people who use a lot of independent concepts about others and people who use only a few.

The first type of research has mostly used the cue trait and semantic differential methods. The two methods produce similar results and most studies have found three factors, in group data, and these sets of factors are very similar, although they have been given different names. The semantic differential factors are called 'evaluation', 'potency' and 'activity'. A recent study by Lay and Jackson (1969), using the cue trait method, finds three factors: aggression–social desirability, compulsivity–control and independence–

dependence. Three similar factors have also been extracted from ratings of facial expression: pleasant–unpleasant, attention–rejection and degree of activation (Schlosberg, 1954). However, analyses of ratings of people on facial expressions do not always produce three dimensions. Warr and Haycock (1970) find six factors with an English sample: two evaluation factors, two activity factors and two potency factors.

The significance of these findings is uncertain. It has been suggested that the presence of three factors in a variety of rating data shows that we tend to think about other people in terms of three broad categories, represented by the three general factors. This is true up to a point, and the first and largest factor – evaluation – does have a central place in most people's thinking about others. However, there are several points that should be noted, when we consider these three factors.

In the first place, they are derived from group data – usually from a very large number of people. They therefore represent a statistical summary of the group data, and do not necessarily represent factors that occur in every individual set of ratings (or even any set). Secondly, we should note that the adjectives used on the semantic differential are mostly vague, and some of them, for example, 'fragrant', 'sacred', are not usually applied to people at all. It is possible that the inappropriateness of the adjectives used tends to inflate the correlations between the scales. Thirdly, we may think it a little suspicious that the same three factors should emerge with such regularity from semantic differential studies, whatever is being rated – actual acquaintances, public figures, classes of people in general, facial expressions, general concepts or particular words. This suggests that the semantic differential is not uncovering the three basic sets of association rules used for judging people, but is rather telling us something about the meaning of words in general, that is, that ratings using adjectives tend to correlate and produce three factors.

A considerable amount of research has been reported on individual rule systems and the association between different concepts within them. This research has generally used the repertory grid to determine the number of independent classifications of people the subject has, that is, his individual 'factor structure'. This research has mostly studied the difference between people who have a lot of independent concepts and those who have few. This is sometimes called 'cognitive complexity'; however there is some confusion about the term 'cognitive complexity'. Crockett (1965) uses it to refer to the overall number of concepts used by the subject (regardless of whether they were used in the same way or not) *and* the number of independent concepts, and suggested that the two measures were highly correlated. Little (1968c) shows that they are, in fact, completely uncorrelated. We will therefore, reserve the term 'cognitive complexity' for work that deals with the number of independent classifications the subject makes; this is usually extracted from repertory grids. A number of findings emerge. Extraverts and members of college fraternities are more complex. Women are more complex. Less complex judges see others in 'black and white' terms, and also tend to think that social relations are more 'balanced' than they really are. There is some evidence that complex people can integrate conflicting information about others, although this has not always been replicated. There is no relation between intelligence and cognitive complexity. Less complex judges assume similarity to a greater extent, but are not less accurate than more complex judges.

3. The study of associative inference rules tells us what relationships people expect to find between different items and classes of items of behaviour. Research in personality is concerned with the real relationships between items of behaviour. A comparison of the two sets of data will tell us whether our expectations about the relations between different sorts of behaviour are correct or not.

The comparison is sometimes complicated by the differing

forms taken by scientific and everyday descriptions of personality and behaviour. Most modern approaches to personality insist on a dimensional approach, rather than a typology. Thus every person is placed along an extraversion dimension; people are not divided into separate classes labelled extravert and introvert. However, it seems likely that most rule systems are typological. Indeed, this is an assumption of Kelly's personal construct theory. People classify others as good or bad, neurotic or stable, extravert or introvert. Of course, some thinking about people does use dimensional concepts; people will say that one person is more extraverted than another but not so extraverted as a third. Even so, most thinking about people uses classes rather than dimensions; language itself is very suitable for classifying people and not at all suitable for ranging them on a dimension. Rule systems are predominantly typological because there are limits to the number of distinctions we can make in successive comparisons along one dimension. A personality test, like the Eysenck Personality Inventory, can distinguish twenty-four different levels of extraversion, whereas a human judge probably could not distinguish more than four or five.

Individual rule systems are sometimes called 'implicit personality theories', because the subject, without necessarily being aware of it, tends to expect that certain characteristics will be associated. Wiggin, Hoffman and Taber (1969) have recently reported a very ingenious and interesting study on rule systems, or implicit personality theories of intelligence. The judges were presented with case histories of college students, in which a number of items of biographical data were systematically varied; the judges were asked to estimate the student's intelligence. Two-thirds of the judges used vocabulary and school achievement as the main criteria; these were in fact the most accurate indicators. A substantial minority used social status and industriousness, which are less accurate criteria; these subjects tended to be authoritarian in outlook. A few judges used quite irrational criteria; for example one judge assumed that the sole criterion of high intelligence was emotional *in*stability. Indeed many implicit personality theories are incorrect most or all of the time. Chelsea (1965) found that five girls all had quite different implicit personality theories when they were asked to rate ten other girls on five dimensions. For example, one girl assumed a negative correlation between 'empiricism' and 'calmness', while another assumed the two qualities were positively correlated. The five girls all thought 'boldness' and 'extraversion' were positively correlated, but to varying extents. In fact, all five girls were wrong for all five traits, since the traits are all quite unrelated.

Several theories have been developed to account for the way in which people seek consistency in their thoughts and attitudes. Although not entirely satisfactory, these theories (see Brown, 1965, for a review) are useful when considering personality judgements and implicit personality theories.

Gollin (1954) showed judges films of a girl who behaved both promiscuously and kindly. Many judges found the two facets of her personality inconsistent, that is, counter to their implicit personality theories. Gollin classified their reactions to the inconsistency. Half ignored one of the characteristics and described the girl as kind or promiscuous, but not both. The rest admitted both characteristics, some trying to explain how they were related and some not.

4. We have seen that people expect different attributes to be associated, so that the possession of one trait implies the possession of another. We have also mentioned that people expect their ideas to be consistent. It follows that a change in one aspect of a description or impression of another may lead to other changes. If the judge thinks that 'warm' people are also 'sociable', then changing 'warm' to 'cold' in the judge's information about the person, will affect his judgement of 'sociable' also. The prediction is correct; changing one part of a description of a person usually leads to changes in other logically unrelated parts of the subject's impression. However Asch (1946) suggests that some attributes were more 'central' than others; thus changing these attributes

leads to a series of changes, while changing others does not. For example, altering 'warm' to 'cold' affected the overall impression, while altering 'polite' to 'blunt' has little or no effect on the other dimensions. Certain dimensions are central to the impression, according to Asch's study, while others are not, although the effect depends on the circumstances to some extent.

The central dimension that affects judgements on all other dimensions is most often an evaluative dimension; if the person is liked, favourable characteristics are attributed to him and, if he is disliked, unfavourable characteristics. This is called the 'halo' effect and is a consistent feature of the way most people make their judgements.

Following Asch's initial study with lists of adjectives and ratings, a great number of similar studies have been done. The effects of presenting different combinations of adjectives, in different orders, etc., has been examined in great detail, and theoretical models of 'impression formation' developed (Anderson, 1965). Most work in this area suggests that all attributes have an approximately equal weight in determining the overall impression, whereas Asch's findings suggest that some are more important than others (see Warr and Knapper, 1968, for a review of this area of research). This type of experiment can be criticized for its artificiality – we do not generally receive information in the form of lists of adjectives. Moreover, it has been found that such lists are very sensitive to minor variations, which suggests that their external validity – their application to actual perception – cannot be very high.

Systematic biases

We have already seen that many associative rules are factually incorrect and presumably tend to make the judge form incorrect judgements. There are also several systematic biases in most people's rule systems that further tend to produce incorrect judgements.

One of these is the tendency to assume intentionality. Although many acts are not intentional or are not intended to have the effects they produce, there is a tendency to assume that people always intend to do what they do and intend it to have the effect it has.

This is particularly true of children, who tend to explain every event by attributing an intention to someone (Piaget, 1932): for example, they explain nightfall by saying that the sun has decided not to shine any more or is being prevented from doing so by some more powerful agent. However, while children tend to explain events by ascribing intentions, they do not take intention into account when assessing the wrongness of an action; instead they base their judgements on the damage the act caused. Thus, a child who breaks six cups accidentally is seen as naughtier than one who breaks one cup deliberately. Children begin to acquire adult conceptions of intention at about the age of ten. However, Walster (1966) shows that even adults tend to judge the wrongness or culpability of acts by their outcomes, to some extent. The more serious the consequences of an accident – for example, as a result of a car running away down a hill – the more likely people were to say that it was the driver's fault for not checking his brakes more often, etc. A classic study by Thibaut and Riecken (1955) shows that the assumption of intentionality is related to status. A high status and a low status person were shown being persuaded to give blood; the subjects saw the high status person as volunteering, while the low status person was seen as being coerced. Free will is apparently seen as the prerogative of high status people (see Maselli and Altrocchi, 1969, for a review of the research).

There is a tendency for even inanimate objects to be ascribed intentions; children and people from primitive cultures tend to do this. Even civilized adults can attribute intentions to inanimate objects; Heider and Simmel (1944) made cartoon films of geometrical shapes moving about and found that people saw these objects in human terms, having intentions, etc. (This may have been a metaphorical interpretation however.) Certainly people tend to attribute intentions to animals; much of this is mere anthropomorphism, yet Hebb (1946) reports that he was unable to describe the behaviour of his chimpanzees except in terms of organized and purposeful actions.

A second source of bias in perception of others is assumed liking and assumed similarity. Our judgements of other people's characteristics are not impartial, but often tend to reflect what we would like, rather than what is actually true. They are systematically biased as a result. There are several theories of cognitive balance, for example, Heider (1958), that postulate that we expect certain relations between other people, ourselves, our ideas and other people's ideas. We expect the people we like to like us and to share our views. We expect the people we dislike to dislike us and reject our views. More complex predictions have been made: for example, that we expect our enemies to dislike our friends and vice versa; however these do not always hold true. Tagiuri (1958) finds that some of these predictions are correct; there is a very strong tendency – not always justified – to assume that other people reciprocate our feelings of liking towards them.

There is a third, rather similar source of bias, called 'projection'. The judge's perception of others is clouded and made inaccurate by his own needs and motivations. Projection was originally a Freudian concept: unacceptable characteristics in the judge are ascribed to others, as a defence mechanism. However, the concept has become rather diffuse and covers several different processes; Murstein and Pryer (1959) distinguish various meanings of the term, in their valuable review. 'Attributive projection' is better known as 'assumed similarity' and refers to the tendency already discussed, to assume others are like oneself. 'Classical projection' refers to Freudian projection: the judge attributes his own unacceptable characteristics to others, to avoid admitting to himself that he has them or has them to an unusual degree. The judge will attribute to others a higher degree of undesirable characteristics, and attribute to himself a lesser degree than he really has. Classical projection, therefore, differs from assumed similarity in two respects. Firstly, only undesirable traits will be attributed to others and, secondly, the judge will not attribute them to himself. Unfortunately assumed similarity effects make it hard to find evidence of projection.

Sears (1936) finds some evidence for projection of meanness in students, but the tendency was not very large and could have been an assumed similarity effect since desirable traits were 'projected' as well. Two studies have produced evidence of projection and may not be affected by assumed similarity artefacts since they have an external criterion. Weingarten (1949) finds that judges who attributed emotional problems to other people tended to have a history of such problems themselves. Similarly, Zimmer (1955) finds that judges attributed those traits to a disliked photo that they themselves experienced conflict over; the criterion of 'conflict' was a word association test, not the judge's report. The judges attributed non-conflictful traits to the photo they liked. These two studies are suggestive but not conclusive.

Murstein and Pryer distinguished a third type of projection, which they call 'rationalized projection'. The judge attributes thoughts, etc., to another, and is aware of doing so, but does not realize *why* he does so. A study by Frenkel-Brunswik (1939) may help to illustrate it. Students at the University of Vienna wrote biographies and gave their opinions about their conduct and principles, and about any changes in the university they thought necessary. They were also rated by two other students and two university staff members. Frenkel-Brunswik found some significant relations between the students' attitudes and opinions and the judges' opinions. For example, students who complained that the teaching at the university was not good enough were rated as lacking in ability by the judges. These students seemed in fact to be blaming their shortcomings on the environment. (Obviously these findings could be explained differently: possibly the judges knew that a particular student thought the teaching poor and so explained this by claiming that he was lacking in ability. However, this is still evidence for rationalized projection but on the part of the judges, not the subjects.)

Rationalized projection occurs frequently in everyday life, and can be explained very easily. For example, Frenkel-Brunswik's students were presumably not doing well in their courses, since they complained about them. If they admitted that the courses were not at fault they would have had to admit that some of the reason for their failure lay in themselves; it was simpler for them to believe that the fault lay in the courses. The same analysis applies if the judges, in Frenkel-Brunswik's study, were the ones who were projecting.

Stability and rigidity

We have seen that many association rules are incorrect: for example, mental instability is not a good criterion for intelligence. It follows that judges who use incorrect inference rules will be unlikely to make accurate judgements. As we emphasize in chapter 6, judgements are usually made for some purpose and tend to determine the judge's behaviour. If they are incorrect, the judge's behaviour will be inappropriate. On this argument, incorrect association rules will eventually be abandoned when the judge realizes that they are not useful. The Kelly Personal Construct Theory and the social skill model both emphasize the 'adaptive' role of person perception and imply that inference rules will change in the light of experience. However, there is considerable evidence that impressions are often impervious to change. Thus H. H. Kelley (1950) told half a class that a speaker would be warm and the other half that he would be cold; the people who had expected him to be cold, saw him as cold, and they participated less in the group discussion. Their impression of him was to some extent rigidly held and was not altered by subsequent evidence. A similar study by Luchins (1959) finds that the first of two conflicting descriptions of a boy determined the final impression, and the second aspect was ignored. However, he did find that the primacy effect – an example of rigidity – could be abolished by warning the subjects against 'first impressions' or by giving them an intervening task. There is also evidence that 'dynamic' judgements are sometimes rigid. Stanton and Baker (1942) asked interviewers to obtain certain information from subjects, and told them the 'correct' answers beforehand; the interviewees actually gave quite different responses, but the interviewers still reported that they gave the 'correct' answers. Kahn and Cannell (1957) studied recordings of interviews and found that the interviewers had their ideas about what the subject meant to say, and ignored or interrupted him if he tried to explain what he really meant.

There is also research on the rigidity of inference rules themselves. Bonarius (1965) reviews the evidence on stability and change in personal constructs and finds that they do change under certain circumstances. Thus Bieri (1953) finds that the judge's concept of another person changes on greater acquaintance, in the direction of assumed similarity. Lundy (1956) finds the same, but also finds a further change in concepts about another person after several weeks' acquaintance: assumed similarity decreased again. Other studies have shown that both psychotherapy and being at university make people alter their construct systems. Deliberate invalidation of a person's constructs also led to a change.

Rigidity in interpersonal perception can often be explained by cognitive consistency theories. If the subject changes his belief about one thing, he may then have to change his opinion on a whole range of other topics, to maintain consistency. It may be simpler for him to ignore the discrepant information.

So far we have been considering rigidity in interpersonal perception and have implied that rigidity is undesirable. However, our ideas about other people need some stability to allow us to make consistent judgements. Recent work by Bannister (1962), using a version of the repertory test, shows that schizophrenics have disorganized construct systems, so that they cannot make consistent and useful classifications of the people they meet. Bannister calls this the 'serial invalidation' hypothesis, because he suggests that the schizophrenic's early experiences are such that expectations about how people will behave are always invalidated.

Origins of associative rules

We have seen that some rules are correct, but many are not: that people differ in the number of concepts they use to describe others, and in the number of independent dimensions needed to describe their concepts: and that the content of associative rules varies from person to person and, more systematically, as a function of age and sex. We have not yet discussed how people acquire associative rules. A satisfactory explanation of their origin could answer many important questions – for example, why many rules are incorrect and why they are not changed.

Sarbin, Taft and Bailey (1960) list four main sources of rules: induction, construction, analogy and authority. Their discussion, and hence our discussion, is largely speculative, for there is little satisfactory research on this question.

'Induction' means experience. If the judge has consistently observed that people who are intelligent do well at school, then he has learned this rule from experience. Providing his observations were accurate, and based on adequate samples, the rule will be correct.

The same does not apply to rules acquired by 'construction', that is, those that the judge invents for himself. Thus some people think that no woman can be trusted. Such ideas often have no foundation in reality, or even in the judge's experience: the judge has 'constructed' them. Sarbin *et al.* do not explain why people should invent false ideas about others, but an explanation can easily be supplied. Such ideas are probably defence mechanisms: for example, the man who thinks women untrustworthy may be rationalizing his unsuccessful relations with women. If 'constructed' ideas about others do satisfy some such need in the judge, they will be highly resistant to change.

Sarbin, Taft and Bailey also include, as 'constructions', deductions from theories, including scientific theories. If a theory allows the deduction that racially prejudiced people are less stable than the norm, the idea is said to be constructed. It might be better to distinguish between irrational constructions, that will generally be wrong, and deductions from theories, that will be correct, if the premises are correct; it would certainly be more flattering to scientific psychology to distinguish its theories from irrational inventions.

The third source of ideas about others is 'analogy'. The judge reasons that because one person reacts in a particular way, everyone else or everyone in a particular class will do the same. Models for analogy include the judge's family, friends, teachers and, most important of all, the judge himself. There is a strong tendency to assume others think and behave like oneself, and in the absence of better information this is a sensible strategy. Analogy with other people is conceptually the same as induction, except that ideas are based on a more limited sample. Some research has been done on analogy within the family, under the rubric of 'identification'. The child adopts the parents' beliefs and attitudes, including possibly the parents' reactions to other people. The literature on identification is reviewed by Secord and Backman (1964).

The fourth and final source of ideas about others is 'authority'. We are told that 'people who are X are also Y' and accept it. This is a large and very important source of ideas or rules about others, particularly for evaluative or normative judgements. Most ideas about what is wrong or unacceptable behaviour come from parents, school friends, workmates, possibly in that order of importance. Much research has been done on the moral development of children, showing at what age they first acquire ideas about right and wrong and how they apply them. Much work has also been done on group norms, that is, shared beliefs about correct behaviour, opinions and attitudes, in family, social and work groups (see Krech, Crutchfield and Ballachey, 1962, for a review). We also get more general ideas about personality, behaviour, moods, etc., from others, in the shape of gossip, and this extends our knowledge of others farther than we could by our own observation. We get additional knowledge about others from books, cinema and television.

4 The Information we Use to Help us Judge

According to the inferential model of interpersonal perception that we considered in chapter 2, we base our judgements of other people on two types of rules – association rules that tell us which attributes or traits are associated, and identification rules that tell us how to recognize people who have particular attributes. Whenever we form a judgement of someone, we use an identification rule to place them in some category or on some dimension. This chapter will be looking at the sorts of information we use to decide what we think about people, and will also evaluate their usefulness, for many identification rules, like many association rules, are incorrect. A considerable amount of research has been done on identification rules, but it has not always been done as systematically as the research on association rules. Many of these research workers have not regarded themselves as working on interpersonal perception, but on non-verbal communication or non-verbal cues. Their research is nevertheless very relevant.

This chapter will be in three parts. The first will discuss methods of studying identification rules; the second will discuss the various types of information available to the judge; and the third will consider what is known about the use made of each and the veridicality of each. There will be a greater emphasis on veridicality or correctness of identification rules, since it is generally easier to establish whether an identification rule is correct than an association rule. Possibly for this reason there has been more research on veridicality of identification rules than on the rules themselves, that is, more research on the 'real' significance of particular items of information than on the meaning people give them.

Some identification rules have received a lot of attention as 'stereotypes'. Stereotypes are widely held identification rules that concern large, readily recognizable classes of people, for example, workers, Negroes, Jews, Young Conservatives. The term 'stereotype' is also sometimes used to refer to widely held views about the characteristics belonging to people with particular facial features or particular voices. Stereotypes have three characteristics. In the first place, they are very commonly wrong all or most of the time, for example, 'Jews are grasping and clannish', 'people whose eyebrows meet in the middle are murderers'. Secondly, they tend to be viewed overinclusively or to be rigidly held. Thus the person who thinks 'Jews are grasping and clannish' takes it to mean 'all Jews and only Jews are etc.'; he also refuses to recognize exceptions when he encounters them. Thirdly, stereotypes often divide people up in ways that are felt to be inappropriate; it is thought that we should not make judgements – especially incorrect ones – about people because they are Jewish or manual workers, etc.

Methods of studying identification rules

The research on association rules, described in the previous chapter, used self-report or 'paper and pencil' methods; these methods have also been used to study identification rules, although there are doubts about their suitability. There are two reasons for this. Firstly, the subject may not always be willing to describe his identification rules if he thinks they are discreditable or likely to be regarded as foolish. This is particularly true where the subject makes inferences about others on the basis of their race or colour.

The second problem in using verbal report methods to study identification rules is more serious. The subject may not know what his identification rules are, or he may think he knows what they are, but in fact give an incorrect report. Some identification rules involve subtle details of non-verbal behaviour that may not be open to introspective reports; indeed Goffman (1956) suggests that there may be a positive taboo on discussing it. It follows that we could not give an accurate account of the reasons that lead us to conclude that someone dislikes us or is impatient to leave. Maier and Jantzen (1967) report some interesting studies on the cues used in judgements of honesty, and conclude that the reasons the judges gave for their judgements were not trustworthy, since accurate and inaccurate judges gave the same reasons. In subsequent work, Maier has not used verbal reports for he considers them likely to be rationalizations.

Where verbal report methods cannot be used, one of two other methods must be used instead. A standard message can be systematically varied to see whether the judge responds to changes. For example, hesitations can be inserted into a recorded utterance to see whether this alters the hearer's judgements of the speaker's anxiety. Alternatively the message can be presented by various combinations of channels – for example, visual and auditory separately, and together – to determine what effects these variations have. Thus Ekman (1965) has presented judges with photos of the subject's head only, body only and head and body together, and studied their ratings of various emotions in the subject. The results suggest that facial expression identifies the emotion while body cues indicate its intensity.

The information available to the judge

An identification rule says how a particular type of person may be recognized. It states that people who have a specified physical characteristic, or who behave in a particular way, have a particular attribute. The distinguishing characteristics of different types of people may be considered under three headings – as follows.

Content

Content refers to the subject's actions and utterances, what he says and does. It is easy to overlook this source of information because it is so obvious. The simplest way of obtaining many sorts of information is to ask the subject. The information obtained in this way has the advantage of being very explicit; the judge does not have to interpret it, as he does the subject's actions and non-verbal expression. However, information direct from the subject cannot always be relied on; people try to present themselves in the best possible light. This is called the 'social desirability effect' and it makes many personality questionnaires very hard to interpret. Thus it may be unsafe to rely on the subject's verbal report on topics involving his self-esteem, although his report on more neutral topics may be reliable. It is sometimes possible to avoid the social desirability problem by carefully phrased questions, however.

The subject's actions are also an important source of information and, for some judgements, they are the only reliable criterion. For example, it is no use relying on what the subject says, when estimating his honesty or trustworthiness; nor can a confident and sincere manner always be taken at its face value. The criterion of honesty is the absence of dishonest behaviour. However, the subject's behaviour is not usually as explicit as his utterances. The judge must observe and interpret it, and systematic biases may creep in. For example, some experiments described in the previous chapter showed that people often assume acts to be deliberate and intentional when they are not. It is also worth noting that attitudes and behaviour are not always consistent; the subject may say one thing and do another. A well-known study by Kutner, Williams and Yarrow (1952) shows that restaurant owners' stated policy of not serving non-white people was not put into practice when non-whites actually came to the restaurant.

Context

The second source of information is the context of the subject's behaviour. For example, discussing cricket scores in church would be rather outrageous, whereas discussing them at a party would be conventional, even rather dull behaviour. No action can be evaluated unless its context is taken into account. The absence of any context is one of the reasons why laboratory experiments often seem artificial. Secord and Backman (1961) point out that the situation the person is in – the role he is filling – often determines his behaviour, rather than his personality. Knowing *where* the person is may be more informative than knowing *who* he is.

The subject's utterances and actions, and the context in which they occur, may be witnessed directly by the judge, or he may know about them at second hand, by report or from memory. When the judge reaches a conclusion about the subject, he will take into account things the subject said and did on previous occasions. His judgements may also be affected by what others have told him about the subject. Second-hand information about people – formally presented, as in references or testimonials, or informally presented, as in everyday gossip – plays a large part in determining the impressions formed of new acquaintances. It is also likely to be a very unreliable source of information. Indeed, some judgements can be positively irrational; two studies have shown that people who have undesirable names, by US standards, are attributed undesirable characteristics and are actually more unpopular. Objective items of information – age, occupation, events in the subject's past – may be communicated accurately, but judgements about the subject's personality are more likely to reflect the judge's biases than to convey any accurate information on the subject.

Non-verbal expression

The third source of information about the subject is his non-verbal expression, and the greater part of the research to be reported has studied this. 'Non-verbal expression' covers a wide variety of behaviour, but a distinction between 'static' and 'dynamic' cues may be made. Static cues do not change during the encounter, while dynamic cues do. (The distinction is not the same as that between static and dynamic judgements.)

Non-verbal cues may be classified as follows:

Static
face
physique
voice
clothes and other man-made adornments, e.g. spectacles
make-up
hair style

Dynamic
orientation
distance
posture
gesture
diffuse body movement
facial expression
gaze direction
tone of voice
rate, amount and fluency of speech

(It is important to distinguish between 'face' and 'facial expression', and 'voice' and 'tone of voice'. Thus 'voice' refers to enduring characteristics of the subject's voice – its loudness, harshness, etc., regional accent, etc. – whereas 'tone of voice' refers to variations in the pitch, volume, etc., of the voice, that occur continuously while the person is speaking.)

Review of the literature on the various sources of information

In this review we will consider each type of information in turn, and discuss what use is made of it, that is, what identification rules are widely held, and how useful the information is, that is, whether it is veridical or not.

T–IP–C

Content

Numerous studies of the accuracy of perception show that the subject's actions and utterances affect the impression others form of him, and that second-hand information can also affect judgements of him. The operation of systematic biases – social desirability and attribution of intentionality – have already been mentioned. A number of interesting studies have recently examined the relative importance of content and non-verbal expression, in various types of judgement. Argyle, Salter, Burgess, Nicholson and Williams (1970) find that the non-verbal elements of a message about the subject's attitude to the judge carries far more weight than the content of the message. On the other hand, two studies find that visual information is not much used (Giedt, 1955) or is positively unhelpful (Maier and Thurber, 1968), when judges were rating personality characteristics of the subjects. It appears that non-verbal information is necessary for some sorts of judgements, but not for others; Argyle *et al.* (1970) suggest that interpersonal attitudes are conveyed non-verbally and there is a taboo on expressing them verbally.

Little has been reported on content alone. Giedt (1955) finds that inaccurate judgements by psychiatrists tend to result from a failure to take what the subject says at its face value. Rather they 'interpret' it in terms of 'reaction formation' and so on, and so come to the wrong conclusions. There is also some evidence from studies of selection interviews, that will be discussed in a later chapter.

Context

A few studies have been reported on the effect of context. An ingenious study by Holmes and Berkowitz (1961) shows that judgements of the pleasantness of a subject show a contrast effect. If the judge has previously seen a very unpleasant person, a pleasant person seems even more pleasant. A judge's opinion of someone to some extent depends on what he is used to. A study by Mintz (1956) shows that the impersonal environment can also affect the impression the subject creates. A subject seen in a pleasant room is rated differently to a subject seen in an unpleasant room. However, the effects of context may be far more complex; a class study by the author, using different musical backgrounds to a standard speech by the subject, produced confusing results, quite unlike those predicted, since the judges interpreted the backgrounds in unexpected ways.

Non-verbal expression – static features

Face. The subject's face, at rest, conveys a variety of information, mostly rather superficial. It reveals the subject's racial origins but probably not his nationality. It reveals his age within limits, and sex, although judgements of sex might not be completely reliable based on the face alone, without the information from hair style, make-up, etc. However, it seems unlikely that the face reveals much about more important things such as personality or intelligence. It has been suggested that if a person habitually assumes a particular expression, which may be indicative of his personality, this will affect the skin and muscles and leave identifiable traces; there is no evidence of this however. The face does convey one essential piece of information – the identity of the person.

It appears that the face has little cue value, but people make many inferences about others from their faces. Secord (1958) presented subjects with still photos of people and asked them to describe their personalities; the subjects did so readily and their descriptions were often uniform, suggesting that there are facial stereotypes, that is, widely held identification rules relating appearance to personality. For example, girls with bowed lips were generally seen as demanding and also as promiscuous. Swarthy complexions were disliked and their owners attributed undesirable characteristics. An earlier study by Brunswik and Reiter (1937) finds stereotyped ideas about intelligent and dull faces. These stereotypes are unlikely to have any validity, although there may be a self-validation effect, such as people with 'ugly' faces becoming unpopular, resenting this and thus becoming disagreeable. It is not surprising that the face at rest should convey little useful information, since the person has very little control over it, and it cannot reflect his personality, etc., in any way.

Physique. Several typologies of physique have been devised and some include ideas about personality traits associated with different physiques, but these have only limited validity; it follows that physique is unlikely to be a useful index of any important characteristics. Strongman and Hart (1968) produce some evidence on stereotyped ideas about physique, showing that we expect fat people to be jolly, thin people to be nervous, muscular people to be energetic, etc.

Voice. A considerable number of studies have been reported on the information conveyed by the voice, and its accuracy (see Kramer, 1963, for a review). It is possible to identify the speaker's national or regional origins by his accent, often with some precision. It is also possible to identify class and occupation. One early study found that actors and clergy were particularly easy to identify, but also found some systematic errors in judgements, showing that the judges had stereotyped ideas about some professions. Age can be estimated reliably from the voice and, rather surprisingly, so can physique. The evidence on less superficial characteristics is not so impressive. One study found a low positive correlation between actual intelligence and estimates made from the subject's voice. Some studies have found that personality can be judged from the voice, while others have found that judges agreed about the subject's personality, but were quite wrong, showing that there are stereotyped ideas about the voice. Another study found that leadership potential could not be estimated from the voice; again the judges agreed about leadership, but were quite wrong. An unpublished study by Lalljee (1967) looks at vocal stereotypes in a new way. Judges were asked to rate four different voices, speaking neutrally; it was found that some voices were rated as sounding more anxious or more bored than others. These 'base levels' may affect the interpretation of the subject's moods, etc.

The voice gives more useful and more reliable information about the subject than his face, and judges seem to be able to use this information correctly to some extent, although their rules about the characteristics linked with different voices are sometimes systematically incorrect. The greater accuracy is not surprising since the voice is more easily controlled than the face, and so more likely to reflect individual differences.

Clothes, make-up, hair, etc.

Comparatively little work has been reported on the meaning of these, possibly because they are felt to be too ephemeral and determined by fashion. Thornton (1944) discovers that people wearing glasses are perceived as more intelligent, but does not report whether this perception is correct. A later study by Argyle and McHenry (1971) finds that this effect does not occur if the judge is given a larger sample of the subject's behaviour. This shows that studies on the interpretation of facial features, voice, etc., that give only this information, are probably overestimating their importance. If the judge is given a larger sample of more relevant information – as would normally be the case – he does not allow the subject's appearance to influence his judgement. Two studies report that females who wear lipstick are perceived differently from those who do not; McKeachie (1952) finds that they were perceived as more frivolous, less conscientious and more overtly interested in men and also rather oddly, as more anxious and introspective. Gibbins (1969) finds that teenage girls have very definite ideas about the type of people who would wear particular clothes, and that this goes beyond a simple evaluation to include detailed predictions of behaviour.

It is obvious that clothes, hair style, etc., are highly significant cues, although no systematic research has been reported on their meaning. They are more controllable than any other cue, and are probably used by the subject as a means of telling others how he sees himself and how he wants others to see him. This in turn gives information about the subject's age, class, occupation, group membership and, more especially, about his attitudes and beliefs. To take a very crude example, a man of about twenty who has a beard and long hair is unlikely to express racial prejudice, or vote Conservative, or believe that the nation 'needs more discipline'.

Non-verbal expression – dynamic cues

Most of the work on dynamic non-verbal cues has concentrated on identifying their expressive function during interaction, rather than on finding out what use is actually made of them. It is typically found that any one cue seems to give a variety of signals about the person's mood or state of mind, his attitude to others present, his attitude to what he himself is saying, or about the encounter itself. Most of the research has restricted itself to interactions between two people, since non-verbal signalling in groups is much more complicated.

Orientation. When two people are interacting, they can stand or sit at various angles to each other: head on, side by side, at right angles, or at various oblique angles. Numerous studies have examined the conditions under which various angles are chosen, and have reached a number of conclusions. (See Sommer, 1967, for a review.) Sommer studies the type of encounter the subject anticipates and discovers that pairs of people choose different positions according to whether they are expecting a conversation, a cooperative encounter, a competitive encounter or no encounter at all. Later work (e.g. Cook, 1970) finds that people expecting friendly or intimate encounters choose positions allowing more proximity or even physical contact, whereas people expecting unfriendly encounters choose positions opposite each other, where they could see each other more clearly. These findings show that the choice of position can indicate to the subjects what type of encounter to expect.

A further series of studies showed that status and leadership in a group is related to choice of position and that it is possible to make an informed guess about who is influential, by studying the positions the group members have chosen. It has been found that people in positions having visual control of the group are more likely to assume leadership of the group, although it is not certain whether the position itself gives such an advantage that the person in it becomes leader, or whether those subjects who are used to taking control know the best position to sit in. Another study found that subjects expected high status people to sit at the head of the table, that is, in a position of visual control. In fact, it is not necessary to know the exact processes involved to be able to say that choice of position in a group can be a good index of the relative influence of the members.

Work on the orientation of people who are standing has also found that status affects choice of orientation. (See Mehrabian, 1969, for a review.) Mehrabian finds that his subjects stood obliquely to someone of lower status, and also that they interpreted standing obliquely as a cue to the status of the person. Scheflen (1964) makes some interesting observations on the use of orientation to indicate group boundaries: there is a 'book-ending effect', with the subjects at the ends of the group turning inwards to close off the group.

To conclude, orientation is mostly used to indicate the nature of the encounter and the relations between the group members, although there are slight personality differences. Sommer's and Mehrabian's work show that people use orientation as a cue to group relations.

Distance. A lot of research has also been reported on the related question of the distance two people sit or stand from each other. Hall (1964) suggests that there are four distances at which people interact, corresponding to four types of encounter. Intimate friends interact at a distance of nought to eighteen inches, casual friends at thirty to forty-eight inches, people in social-consultative encounters interact at four to twelve feet, while any distance greater than twelve feet indicates a 'public' encounter. No evidence has been produced to support this, except a study by Sommer which finds that distance varies according to the room the encounter takes place in. This suggests that perhaps Hall's hypotheses need modifying or possibly that distance should be studied in the field and not the laboratory. Several laboratory studies report that subjects stand a little closer to people they like, although the effect is not very great. Several studies have also reported that extraverts stand a little closer than introverts. However, a study by Porter, Argyle and Salter (1970) finds that judges draw no conclusions at all from distance; possibly the variations that occur as a function of liking and extraversion are not noticed, especially as they are very slight compared with the large individual differences in preferred distance Porter, Argyle and Salter find. It is also worth noting that Porter *et al.* studies distance relatively unobtrusively, whereas many other studies have used direct verbal report methods. To conclude, the distance people place themselves apart for interaction is surprisingly uninformative.

Posture, gesture and body movement. 'Posture' refers to the way the person sits or stands, while 'gesture' refers to specific movements. 'Body movement' refers to the overall frequency of gestures and changes in posture. Comparatively little systematic work has been done on these cues. Until recently most work tried to associate particular gestures and postures with emotional states, or to assign a meaning to particular gestures. This is not the best approach, for gestures, and indeed non-verbal behaviour generally, cannot necessarily be translated in this way.

Ekman and Friesen (1969) distinguish five functions of non-verbal cues. Some are 'emblems' – signals that are given deliberately and which have a specific meaning that can be translated directly into words. Typical 'emblems' are shaking the fist to indicate anger, nodding the head to show assent, beckoning, pointing, and so on. These have a communicative significance just like words. Some non-verbal behaviour indicates the emotional state of the person. Ekman and Friesen consider that the face is the main channel for 'affect displays', but gesture and posture play some part as well. Ekman (1965) and Sainsbury (1955) show that anxiety or stress produces identifiable changes of posture and frequency of movement, that can be detected by observers. Ekman also suggests that the body indicates the intensity of the emotion while the face identifies it.

Ekman's next two categories correspond to two of the types of judgement or response listed in chapter 1 – the subject's response to what the other person is saying and the subject's attitude to what he himself is saying. Most people make gestures and movements all the time they are speaking and these movements illustrate what they are saying. Some of the 'illustrators' – as Ekman and Friesen call them – mark off the successive parts of what the speaker is saying and could be thought of almost as a system of visual punctuation, while others expand and clarify the content, indicating spatial relationships, drawing the object mentioned, pointing to the object, or to the speaker's relationship to it, and so on. A recent paper by Kendon (1968) examines the use of such non-verbal accompaniments to speech and finds that the speaker's movements do, in fact, correspond to the structure of what he says, with a hierarchy of movements in different areas paralleling a hierarchical structure of what he says. Thus shifts in the trunk or legs only occur at the ends of paragraphs, while movements of the hands and forearm tend to occur at every phrase. Kendon also finds occurrences of movements associated with the content of speech, as well as its structure: pronouns referring to the speaker are accompanied often by a gesture moving towards the speaker, while other pronouns are accompanied by gestures moving away from the speaker. These movements do not communicate anything in themselves, but probably help the listener attend to and understand what is being said.

Fourthly, somewhat similar movements and gestures are produced by the listener, indicating how he is reacting to the speaker. These 'regulators' have been studied by Scheflen

(1964) and others in a somewhat unsystematic way. Head nods, raising the eyebrows, slight postural shifts can indicate to the speaker that the listener is interested or not, wants him to go faster, or repeat something, or change the subject, or stop. Verbal conditioning studies (see Krasner, 1958) have shown that head nods, as well as verbal equivalents, can make the speaker say more and absence of these can make him say less, but have not studied any of the other, more subtle cues.

Finally, Ekman and Friesen suggest that some gestures occur because they are learned as useful, and have remained part of the subject's behaviour, although they no longer serve any purpose. Such 'adaptors' are, of course, idiosyncratic, so their significance can only be learned by acquaintance with the subject. It is obviously difficult to produce convincing evidence for this class of signal; nevertheless, the hypothesis is very plausible and would help to explain the large individual differences in non-verbal behaviour. A study by Krout (1954) produces some relevant evidence. His subjects were put under stress and then observed, and any gestures they produced were recorded. Krout found that a great variety of gestures were produced, but some quite consistently; and some of these were related to the subject's report of his reaction to the situation. Some of these gestures were probably 'adaptors' and were originally learned as responses to anxiety.

Gestures and shifts in posture convey a variety of information during the encounter about the subject's emotional state, about his reaction to the speaker; they are also used as an accompaniment to what the speaker is saying.

Facial expression. The work on facial expression is discussed in greater detail in chapter 6, since it has mostly concentrated on the accuracy with which we can recognize different emotions. Although most of the work is on the recognition of emotion, some data have been reported on expression. This tends to suggest that emotions are not always expressed in the same way, although the concept of 'display rules' (see page 107) and cross-cultural evidence suggests that certain 'basic' emotions or 'primary affects' are 'programmed' the same way universally, although different cultures have different norms about expressing them. Ekman suggests that the 'basic' emotion may show through, even though suppressed; certainly Haggard and Isaacs (1966) find evidence of 'micro-momentary' expressions – complete changes of facial expression so rapid that slow-motion films are required to detect them. The number of primary affects has been variously estimated as six, seven and eight, but the differences seem to occur only because different investigators may class two emotions as one primary affect, and also because one list excludes 'interest'. In fact, all the lists omit one or possibly two important responses that have been shown to be expressed more consistently than any others – the startle response and the orienting reflex.

There is plenty of evidence that the six, seven or eight basic emotions can be recognized from photos or short films or even from live people. However, the methods have been criticized both for artificiality and for use of unsatisfactory criteria. It is possible that the results from the recognition of emotion studies show no more than that the judges can use certain stereotypes of facial expression, and do not prove that they can identify real facial expressions. One or two studies have examined the recognition of emotional or cognitive states, using more valid methods. Friedman (1967) shows that judges respond to relatively small variations in expression that the subject produces unintentionally, by systematically varying their behaviour in the way that the subject expects it to change. Jecker, Maccoby and Breitrose (1965) find that facial expression alone is no help in deciding whether someone has understood something.

Ekman's classification of types of non-verbal cue, discussed in the previous section, applies equally to facial expression and, indeed, to all non-verbal signals, although different cues are used to various extents for the different types of information. Thus, facial expression conveys emotion far more than posture does. However, it can also give other sorts of information and recent work has concentrated increasingly on this, possibly as a reaction against the sterility of much previous work. Birdwhistell (1968) produces some relatively unsystematic evidence on changes in facial features by the speaker as an accompaniment to what he is saying, and by the listener as a reaction to what he hears. Birdwhistell puts forward a system of 'kinesics' and suggests that there are thirty-three identifiable meaningful variations or 'kinemes' in North America. (The idea of the kineme, which is derived from the 'phoneme', is very useful; obviously not every variation in non-verbal behaviour is meaningful, so it is very important to determine what are the significant variations.) Birdwhistell suggests that the speaker produces 'kinesic stress markers', such as raising of the eyebrows, at the same time as he stresses words vocally; these markers can also be given by gestures. Similar signals are given by the listener, showing how he is reacting to what is being said, and are also, according to Condon and Ogston (1966) correlated with the speaker's movements. Evidently much more research requires to be done on regulators and illustrators. This research should be done more systematically and should be reported in greater detail.

Gaze direction. During an interaction, one person may look at the other in the region of the eyes, or not look at him. Generally he will look some of the time, although there are large individual differences. A study by Kendon (1967) shows that people look for more of the time and in longer gazes while they are listening, and in shorter but more frequent gazes while speaking. The two people will not usually return each other's gaze – meet the other in the eye – for more than a few seconds at a time. Looking at the other has several functions. The most obvious is observation – to see what the other person is like and what he is doing. However, looking is also used to give various signals. These two quite different functions – observation and signalling – make the study of gaze direction rather complicated, since no way has yet been discovered of determining which of the two functions gaze serves at any particular time.

Exline shows that gaze gives a variety of related signals about the looker's attitude towards the other person and to what is being said. The subject looks less at someone he dislikes (Exline and Winters, 1965) and if he finds the topic of conversation difficult or embarrassing (Exline, 1966). Most people look less if they are lying, but very Machiavellian people do not. Mehrabian (1969) reports that people look less at someone of lower status. Work by Kendon (1967) shows that looking also plays an important role in regulating the interchange of speakers. When the speaker is coming to the end of his utterance, he looks up – having been looking away while speaking – and continues to look at the other person, who then starts speaking. If the speaker does not look up at the end of his utterance, the other person takes appreciably longer to respond, suggesting that he was waiting for the usual signal that he should take over. If the speaker pauses, but has not finished his utterance, he does not look up.

Kendon's work shows that people recognize gaze signals when they are given to indicate interchange of speakers, and a recent study by Kendon and Cook (1969) shows that people also recognize gaze signals of like and dislike. Subjects who look at the other person in short but frequent gazes are not liked as much as those who look in longer gazes – a finding that fits in with popular notions about 'steady gazes' and 'shifty-eyed people'. However, it does not follow that long gazes between two people indicate that they are friendly, nor that the recipient of the long gaze will see it as a friendly sign. Argyle and Dean (1965) hypothesize that there is an appropriate level of friendliness for any encounter, that is maintained by the amount of mutual gaze, among other things. Therefore, if one of the subjects wants to make the encounter more intimate, he may look more, but if the other person does not approve of this increase in intimacy, he will not reciprocate and may see the increased gaze as an intrusion. In some circumstances, a long gaze is a positively hostile signal. Exline finds that monkeys attacked a man who stared at them and who did not 'submit' by lowering his gaze. The same thing has been known to happen among humans. To conclude, looking at someone is a sign of interest and attention, and the nature of the attention – friendly, hostile or possibly sexual – depends on the context.

Tone of voice. Comparatively little research has been done on the vocal expression of emotion, possibly because the technical difficulties involved are considerable. The development of the tape-recorder has made recording voices very simple, but analysing pitch and volume and other characteristics of the voice requires complicated apparatus, not commercially available. An early series of studies by Fairbanks and others – described in Kramer (1963) – finds that the volume, fundamental frequency and rate of speech all vary systematically according to the emotion student actors are trying to portray; however, this study is open to the objection that only theatrical stereotypes are being studied. Davitz (1964) finds that some emotions can be consistently rated for their acoustic qualities by expert listeners, but this is a rather unsatisfactory method. Ostwald (1965) uses an objective measuring device – the speech spectrograph – and finds that certain types of voice, in mental patients, can be identified and have some relation to the progress of the patient's illness. However, the method is complicated, since the human voice has a fundamental frequency and a spectrum of overtones; at present it is only possible to analyse a single sound, not continuous speech.

The work on recognition of emotion in speech is described in chapter 6. It is very similar to the work on the recognition of emotion from facial expression. The methods are often artificial and the criteria for the emotional states often dubious. A fair degree of accuracy of identification is found in most cases, but this might reflect only the judge's acquaintance with certain stereotypes. Little has been reported about the recognition of states other than the conventional list of emotions. One study – cited by Kramer (1963) – finds that certainty and uncertainty can be distinguished reliably, while another finds that fatigue cannot be, and is in fact judged with worse than chance accuracy.

Not all variations in tone of voice indicate changes in the emotional state of the speaker, any more than all smiles indicate that the subject is happy or pleased. Many variations in tone of voice are 'illustrators', emphasizing and modifying what the speaker is saying. Linguists have recognized for a long time that there are characteristic patterns of pitch and stress, varying from language to language, that indicate when the speaker is reaching the end of his sentence or utterance, or which indicate that the remark is a question or order, etc. More recently an attempt has been made to systematize the study of such variations, using the Trager–Smith system of 'paralanguage'. This has two parts – pitch, stress and juncture, and various 'modifiers'. These features are coded by the trained listener. Detailed analyses of samples of speech have been produced (for example, by Pittenger, Hockett and Danehy, 1960), showing how paralinguistic changes reflect what the speaker is saying, often in a very subtle way. However, there are serious doubts about the validity of the method. Dittman and Wynne (1961) show that only the pitch, stress and juncture categories can be coded reliably. Liberman (1965) finds that paralinguists tend to code the pitch and stress according to the grammatical structure of the sentence, not independently of it. We may conclude that the paralinguistic system is of limited value and that it would be better to concentrate on devising objective measures of speech.

Rate and fluency of speaking. Several variables are relevant – rate of speech, number and length of pauses, corrections and slips of the tongue and 'filled pauses' ('er', 'um' and similar sounds). Rate of speech is, in fact, largely a function of the number and length of pauses. Pauses occur for several reasons – to allow the speaker to breathe in or out, for emphasis and 'illustration', to provoke a reply (occasionally), and, according to the work of Goldman-Eisler (1968), when the speaker has 'dried up', that is, cannot think what to say next or how to phrase it. A high rate of pauses, particularly when they occur within phrases, indicates that the speaker is thinking hard and having difficulty with his material. Other work has tried to relate rate of speech, and hence of pausing, to anxiety, but the results have been conflicting. A study by the author (Cook, 1969) finds that some speakers increase their speech rate when anxious, while others decrease theirs. An unpublished study by Lalljee and Williams (1967) finds that changes in speech rate are interpreted in various ways by those that hear them, and are not consistently interpreted as indicating anxiety. These studies show that rate of speech and of pausing are good cues to the thought processes of the speaker, but are not reliable signs of anxiety.

Errors in articulation and changes in sentence structure – known as 'speech disturbances' – have been shown to be a function of anxiety in many studies (e.g. Cook, 1969). Lalljee and Williams (1967) find that speech disturbances are interpreted by judges as indicating anxiety. Evidently speech disturbances are a reliable expression of anxiety and are recognized as such by those who hear them. However, the relation of filled pauses to anxiety is not so clear. Some studies have reported that they increase as a function of stress, but others have not found this. The evidence, discussed in detail by Cook (1969), indicates that on the whole they are not signs of anxiety. Subsequent work has tested the hypothesis put forward by Maclay and Osgood (1959) that filled pauses are signals by the speaker that he has not finished, even though he has paused. However, studies by the author and M. G. Lalljee show that they do not increase when the speaker is more liable to interruption (Lalljee and Cook, 1969) and that they are not interpreted by the listener as indicating that the speaker has not finished. In fact, they do not express the speaker's desire to continue speaking, nor are they recognized as such by the hearer. Their function, if any, is still uncertain.

5 How we Test Accuracy of Judgement

This chapter will be rather more technical than the rest of the book. Accuracy of interpersonal perception is a very important issue, yet has presented serious methodological problems. These problems have seemed so serious to many working in the area that the study of accuracy has virtually been abandoned. Indeed, it is now commonly said that accuracy is not a real issue at all; this seems to the author only a rationalization of the failure of research in the area.

This chapter will be in two parts. The first will consider a general model for studying accuracy and the second will describe the various methods that have been employed, in the light of this model, and enlarge on the technical problems involved.

A general model for studying accuracy of perception

When we set out to design an experiment to determine the accuracy with which a particular judgement is made, there are six details to be considered.

1. *Judges.* Firstly we require a set of people to make judgements. The judges may vary in number, as well as in sex, age, personality, etc.

2. *Subjects.* We also require a person or set of persons to be judged. The subject(s) may vary in age, sex, personality, etc.

3. *Sample of subject's behaviour.* In some studies the judges are asked to judge people they already know. In many studies however they are asked to judge people on the basis of a limited sample of behaviour: an interview or discussion, or a photograph, tape-recording, piece of handwriting, etc.

4. *Content of judgement*. The judges can be asked for a variety of different judgements. The possible range is outlined in chapter 1.

5. *Form of judgement*. The judge can be asked to give his opinion in six different ways:

(a) Free description. The judge is allowed to use his own words and his reply is content analysed. This method is rarely used.

(b) Rating scale. The judge gives his judgement in the form of a numerical rating. This method is used most commonly where the judgement concerns personality traits. The judge is in effect being asked to assign a number to the subject, representing the level of a particular trait that subject possesses.

(c) Multiple choice. The judges is asked to choose one of a number of alternatives, to describe the subject or to coincide with the subject's choice. This method has been used very widely.

(d) Ranking. The judge is asked to place a number of subjects in order of their possession of a particular attribute. This method is rarely used.

(e) Sorting. The judge is asked to sort the subjects into a specified number of groups of specified sizes. For example Toch, Rabin and Wilkins (1962) instructed their judges to sort twelve photographs into four Jewish subjects, four Catholic subjects and four Protestant subjects. This method is rarely used.

(f) Matching. The judges are given two sets of samples of behaviour from one set of subjects, and told to match them, that is, sort them into pairs, each pair belonging to one subject. This method has been used very widely.

6. *Criterion*. If we are measuring the accuracy of judgements, we require a criterion, that is, we must know what the 'real' or 'correct' answer is, or at least what we will accept as the 'correct' answer. Judgements of distance, for example, can be checked by measuring the real distance but establishing a criterion for judgements of personality, mood, etc.

often presents problems. There are five ways of establishing a criterion in person perception studies:

(a) 'Face' validity. Some studies have no proper criterion, but assume that a particular answer is correct. For example, many early studies of the recognition of emotion used sets of photographs for which there is no criterion, except the intentions of the person posing for the photographs and the experimenter's approval of his performance.

(b) Expert opinion. In some early studies the experimenter himself decided what the correct answer was or asked some of his colleagues to decide. Obviously this criterion is inadequate unless the experimenter or his colleagues can be proved to be accurate judges themselves.

(c) Ratings by others and group consensus. In some studies ratings of the subjects by people who know him are taken as the criterion. This is valid where the ratings or descriptions concern specific behaviour, but more doubtful where the ratings concern traits or general descriptions of personality. In the latter case we are effectively comparing two independent judgements of the person to determine whether they agree.

In some trait-rating studies the criterion was taken as the average opinion of all the judges. A good theoretical case can be made for this criterion, but from a practical point of view it is not very good since it involves statistical artefacts of a type to be discussed later.

(d) Subject's description of himself. This may be given in various forms. The subject may rate himself or may complete a personality inventory. This criterion assumes that the subject's self-description is accurate and honest. There is also a risk that the judges' task becomes deciding what the subject said in answer to the questions, rather than actually judging his behaviour.

(e) Objective or biographical data. This is an ideal criterion, but is not available for most of the judgements we are considering.

Principal types of study of accuracy of perception

If all the various factors, discussed in the previous section, were systematically varied and combined in every possible combination, there would be a very large range of experimental designs open to the experimenter. However, research in the area has tended to use a limited range of methods: emotion recognition, empathy studies, trait rating and matching studies. We will discuss each method in turn. The first part of each discussion will describe the types of judges, subjects, samples, judgements and criteria used and the second will comment more generally on the problems encountered.

Emotion recognition

Studies of the expression and recognition of emotion have a long history. The first experiments were done by Darwin in 1872, to test his evolutionary theory of emotional expression. The same basic method has been used in numerous studies since.

Judges and subjects. Most studies have used large numbers of judges, but few subjects. Many have used only one subject.

Sample of behaviour. This has generally been very limited. Studies of facial expression have used photographs or drawings and a number of sets of these have been developed: the Rudolph pictures, the Feleky pictures, the Ruckmick pictures, the Frois–Wittman pictures. All these series were posed, generally by actors. Other studies use photos taken 'live' either in real life situations (Munn, 1940) or in contrived laboratory settings (Landis, 1929). A few studies have used 'live' subjects, either adults or infants. Surprisingly few studies have used filmed expressions. The extensive use of photographs of actors is unfortunate. Their expression may not resemble those normally produced by naïve subjects, so that ability to recognize them may only be evidence of knowledge of theatrical conventions or similar stereotypes of expression. Certainly the Frois–Wittman pictures, illustrated in Woodworth (1938), are very artificial and exaggerated.

Studies on vocal expression use three types of material, which control or eliminate content in different ways. In the meaningless content method, the subject recites the alphabet or a list of numbers in the appropriate tone of voice; the effect is rather comic yet the method is widely used, even in recent studies. In the standard content method a sentence is used, for example, 'I'm going out now. I won't be back until later. If anyone calls please take a message', that can be said appropriately in any emotional state. Recently methods have been developed of filtering speech, to make the content unintelligible, while leaving the emotional content intact.

Photographs give the judges only a single 'frozen' expression, although actual facial expressions last and change over time, being a sequence of differing expressions. Photographs probably make the judge's task more difficult and more artificial. The same is true of tape-recordings of meaningless material, which present only one emotion, although they last in time. Short films and 'live' presentations are the best methods.

Content and form of judgement. A few early studies used free descriptions and, more recently, Frijda (1969) has also used them. The majority of studies use multiple choice methods. A typical list of alternatives taken from Thompson and Meltzer (1964) includes: happiness, love, fear, determination, bewilderment, surprise, anger, suffering, disgust, contempt. We commented in chapter 1 on the neglect of more mundane states like irritation, fatigue, etc. A few recent studies have used rating methods.

Criterion. Various criteria have been used. Many studies have used the subject's intention as the only criterion. Other studies used a selection of the material, either those the experimenter thought best or those most consistently identified, so that the criterion was the experimenter's 'expert' opinion or group consensus. Some studies have used photos obtained in known situations. Such photos can be taken in the laboratory; for example, Landis (1929) photographed subjects as they decapitated a rat and received electric shocks. Other studies have used photos taken from the press.

The criteria used are for the most part unsatisfactory, tending to circularity.

General comments. Providing short films are used, together with a sensible list of alternatives for the judge to choose from, studies of the recognition of emotion are quite useful. However, they are somewhat limited. The judgements are made in isolation; the judges do not interact with the subjects. The method also relies on verbal report, whereas many types of judgement of emotion, or other transient states, might not be made consciously. For example, most people probably could not identify an expression of termination of the encounter from a photograph, but would respond appropriately if one occurred in an actual encounter.

Empathy methods

This class of methods is somewhat misleadingly named as we noted in chapter 2. It differs from the trait-rating task in that the judge is given a multiple choice task, rather than a rating task. Taft (1955) suggests that the multiple choice task is 'non-analytic', whereas the rating task is 'analytic'. In the rating task the judge has to consider an aspect of the subject's personality in isolation and assign a number to it, whereas in the empathy task he has only to 'put himself in the other's shoes', and decide how he would respond.

Judges and subjects. In most studies the judges and subjects are separate groups.

Sample. The sample of behaviour given has varied widely. Gage (1952) shows the judges the subject performing simple motor tasks. Cline (1964) and Crow and Hammond (1957) use filmed interviews. In Taft's (1956) study the judges already knew the subjects.

Form of judgements. The judge is required to choose which of two or more alternatives applies to the subject, or was selected by the subject.

Content. A variety of material has been used. The most popular has been the personality inventory; the judge is required to complete the inventory as he thinks the subject would complete it. Adjective check lists have also been used. Crow and Hammond use a 'reticence test'; the judge is given a list of topics and asked to indicate whether the subject would be willing to discuss them or not. Cline (1964) uses a multiple choice sentence completion task. The most interesting variation on the 'empathy' task is Cline's (1964) 'Behaviour Postdiction Test'. This presents the judge with a specific situation and a choice of four responses, for example:

When the interviewee is in a violent argument usually he:

(a) becomes very sarcastic
(b) uses profanity and obscene words
(c) leaves the room or area
(d) strikes his opponent with his fists

The judge has to indicate what response the subject would make. The items are very carefully selected.

Criterion. Where inventories and adjective check lists, etc., are used, the criterion is the subject's self-report. This has the disadvantage that the judge's task tends to become one of deciding what answer the subject would give to the question, not deciding what his actual behaviour would be. The Behaviour Postdiction Test is particularly carefully validated. Two criteria are used: self-report and the report of two other people who know the subject. Cline chooses only those items where all three agree that the subject always responded that way and never responded according to the incorrect alternatives.

General comments. The empathy method appears at first sight to present no difficulties, except slight uncertainty about the judge's interpretation of the task in some cases. However there is a very serious problem, which makes the results of earlier studies hard to interpret and has led to the virtual abandonment of the method. This problem is 'stereotype accuracy'. In the multiple choice judgement task, the judge has to choose one of two or more alternatives for each of a number of subjects; the criterion is usually the subject's self-report. The number of subjects who choose each of the two or more possible responses obviously depends on the subjects themselves; it is not controlled by the experimenter. It can happen, therefore, that a particular answer is selected by more subjects, and is more popular. For example, if there are twenty subjects and four alternative responses, we might find that one answer is chosen by ten subjects and another by only two. Certainly we should not expect every answer to be chosen by precisely five subjects, unless we controlled the material carefully. This variation in the frequency with which the alternatives are selected has serious consequences. The judge who perceives that a particular response is more likely than any other can achieve a high overall accuracy score by checking that item most or even all the time, and he achieves this high score without discriminating between the different subjects at all. Certainly he has made an accurate judgement – that a particular response is the most likely – but it is not the judgement we intended him to make.

As we said, it is unlikely that the possible responses will be selected exactly equally often; unfortunately, there are several good reasons why this should not happen, so that one response will often be significantly more likely than the others. There are three principal reasons: real similarity, social desirability and assumed similarity.

1. *Real similarity.* Most studies have used college students as subjects; obviously a homogeneous sample will be more

likely to give similar answers, raising the likelihood that one alternative will be significantly more frequent than the others.

2. *Social desirability set.* Subjects completing personality inventories tend to present themselves in a favourable light and not to reveal socially unacceptable facts about themselves. If one of the items in a multiple choice judgement task is obviously socially unacceptable or undesirable, the judge who realizes this and does not check that item will achieve a higher accuracy score.

3. *Assumed similarity.* Judges in interpersonal perception tasks tend to assume others are like them (P. E. Vernon, 1964). This is an interesting fact in itself, but complicates the study of accuracy, for it provides another way in which the judge can identify and use a stereotype of the subjects. The assumed similarity effect is a particular problem in studies that investigate similarity between judge and subject as a determinant of accuracy. Hatch (1962) points out that real similarity (between judge and subject), assumed similarity and accuracy of judgement are all mathematically linked. In particular, accuracy is a function of assumed similarity and real similarity. That is, if the judge assumes similarity, and if the judge and subject really are similar, the judge will get a high 'accuracy' score, although he has not accurately perceived the other at all. The same triangular process can occur with liking. If the judge assumes the subject likes him – a common tendency (Tagiuri, 1958) – and if the other really does like him, the judge will appear to have made an accurate judgement.

The assumed similarity or liking effect makes it hard to interpret many studies. For example Dymond, Hughes and Raabe (1952) have pupils in a class rank each other sociometrically and predict the mean ratings given by the rest of the class. They find that accuracy of perception of others' liking correlates highly with popularity – a most interesting and significant finding. However, most students assume that others would like them, so that those who actually are liked (i.e. the popular subjects) appear to have judged correctly, while the unpopular subjects appear to have judged incorrectly; thus the correlation may be spurious and cannot be taken as evidence of a relation between popularity and accuracy of perception.

We should note that assumed similarity effects are *potential* artefacts: subjects do not always assume accuracy, and even when they do they are not always justified in doing so. It has been widely assumed that because results *could* be the result of assumed similarity, they actually are. A study by Taft (1966) finds that friends are judged more accurately than strangers; this can be dismissed as an assumed similarity effect, since it is well known that friends are more like oneself than strangers and it is also known that they are assumed to be more like oneself. However, Taft finds that assumed similarity is higher for friends, but real similarity is not, on this occasion; therefore, his results cannot be dismissed as an assumed similarity artefact. It follows that many studies that have been dismissed as probable assumed similarity or liking artefacts may be genuine too. In fact, it is known that similarity is not assumed in some circumstances. Rokeach (1945) finds that girls did not assume that others are similar to them in rated attractiveness, but place themselves above the average. Fiedler (1964) shows that effective leaders of groups, in some circumstances, tend to assume that others are dissimilar and to differentiate among the group members. Tagiuri (1958) shows that people do not assume similarity in those they dislike, but rather the opposite. Bieri (1953) shows that assumed similarity increases with greater acquaintance, but Lundy (1956) finds that the effect reversed after several weeks' acquaintance. Scodel and Mussen (1953) find that authoritarian judges assume similarity more than non-authoritarians, but are no less accurate in their judgements.

The stereotype accuracy artefacts present a more serious problem than the statistical artefacts – 'Cronbach's components' – that we will discuss in the next section. The basic problem is that some alternatives are more likely than others; one obvious solution is to ensure that all the alternatives are equally probable. Chance and Meaders (1960) try to avoid assumed similarity effects by using only subjects who are different from the judge. This has the disadvantage that we cannot then determine whether similarity of judge and subject is an important factor. The most elaborate attempt to control the material is made by Hatch (1962) who devises a 'Forced Choice Differential Test' that eliminates all artefacts, but needs twenty hours of computer time to do it. In this the judges – who were managers – were asked to judge *which of two* statements about supervisor–subordinate relations *both of two* subordinates *disagreed* with. By careful choice of items it is possible to eliminate all statistical and assumed similarity artefacts. For example, some items are more controversial and so more likely to provoke disagreement, and if the judge can identify these – an instance of stereotype accuracy – he can achieve a good score, without making any judgements about the individuals. This was prevented by equating both items for controversy. On this task judges performed better than chance, and individual differences were found. Furthermore, there was a relation between difficulty of judgement (defined by the extent of disagreement between the subordinates) and accuracy of judgement. Control of material, is however, unlikely to be a successful method, since it is too laborious. It also places artificial restraints on the material. There are many occasions where the various outcomes to be judged are not equally probable; to take an extreme example, the great majority of cheques presented are genuine, but it is still important to detect the small minority that are not.

It is also possible to change the scoring system to control for artefacts. For example, some early studies subtracted real similarity from accuracy scores, so that the more similar the subject, the less credit the judge received for judging him correctly. Cline (1964) points out that this penalizes the judges unfairly; not all accurate judgements of similar subjects are assumed similarity effects. It might be possible to avoid stereotype artefacts by employing a matching task. The judges would be told how many subjects selected each response and instructed to sort the subjects into a specified number of categories of specified size. This would prevent them 'cheating', by checking the most popular response all or most of the time. As a further refinement it might be possible to instruct the judges to estimate the distribution of responses, that is, how many subjects chose each response, as a first step; this could be taken as a stereotype accuracy score.

Trait rating

Studies of this type have also been very popular, although they are not as numerous as studies of the recognition of emotion, possibly because they involve more work.

Judges and subjects. A large number of judges and of subjects have been used in most studies. In many studies all those taking part act as judges and subjects; all the people in a group rate each other.

Sample of behaviour. In some studies 'real' groups were used, so that judges had been acquainted with the subjects for some time. In other studies judges and subject meet to become acquainted before judgements are made. In most studies, therefore, the judges receive a large and uncontrolled sample of the subject's behaviour. Because the sample is uncontrolled, the study cannot be replicated exactly. On the other hand, live encounters are better than films and more controlled samples, since the judge does interact with the subject and can seek the information he requires, as he would in real life.

Form and content of judgement. As the name implies, studies of this type require the judges to rate the subjects numerically, on various traits. For example, Taft (1956) asked his judges to rate the subjects for persuasiveness, social assertiveness, sociability, carefulness, drive and conformity, on five-point scales.

Criterion. Various criteria have been used, none of which are very satisfactory. Some studies use group consensus or 'expert' opinion, and others have used self-report.

General comments. There are two general comments about this method. The first concerns the logical status of traits and the second, artefacts in the rating process.

1. *Logical status of traits*. The assumption underlying the use of trait descriptions is that people's responses to similar or related situations is consistent. When we say a person is 'rigid' we are summarizing previous behaviour and predicting similar behaviour in future. However, it has been found that there is no evidence of such consistency for some classes of behaviour. For example, rigidity in one situation is not related to rigidity in others; Mischel (1968) remarks that 'The conviction that highly generalized traits do exist may reflect in part (but not entirely) behavioral consistencies that are *constructed* by the observers, rather than actual consistencies in the subject's behaviour.' If the trait does not exist, in the sense that there is no corresponding consistency in the subject's behaviour, it becomes meaningless to discuss the accuracy with which this trait is perceived. (There is, however, good evidence that some traits do represent behavioral consistencies, for example, intelligence).

2. *Statistical artefacts*. In trait-rating studies the judge's accuracy is measured and defined as the difference between the judge's rating of the subject, and the criterion rating. The larger the difference score the less accurate the judge is. For example, if the criterion rating for the subject on a particular trait is 6, the judge who gives that subject a rating of 5 is considered more accurate than the judge who gives a rating of 4. In most studies a number of subjects are rated and an overall difference score is obtained. Cronbach (1955) points out that these difference scores are unsatisfactory measures and may not reflect the judge's accuracy of perception. It will be useful to consider a concrete example. Table 1 presents imaginary ratings, by three judges of ten

subjects on 'narrow-mindedness', together with criterion scores. The first judge has a difference score of 20 and is the 'worst' judge, according to the difference. Inspection of his data shows that his ratings are all 2 points lower than the criterion; if this constant error were eliminated, he would be completely accurate. Cronbach calls such constant errors differences in 'level'. Their significance is uncertain. The judge may be actually underestimating the narrow-mindedness of the ten subjects. The constant error may be a 'leniency effect' – a tendency to rate people favourably. It may mean no more than that the judge is uncertain how to use the numerical scale; he may intend 3 to mean the same as the criterion rater meant by 5.

Table 1
Imaginary Data, Representing the Ratings by Three Judges of Ten Subjects, on a Single Trait

Subjects	1 2 3 4 5 6 7 8 9 10	
Criterion rating	5 6 5 4 5 7 4 5 4 5	
Judge 1	3 4 3 2 3 5 2 3 2 3	difference score = 20
Judge 2	5 8 5 2 5 10 2 5 2 5	difference score = 11
Judge 3	5 5 5 5 5 5 5 5 5 5	difference score = 7

The second judge has a difference score of 11, and is thus the second best judge. Inspection of the data shows that he has correctly identified the mean score as 5, and has correctly perceived that subjects 1, 3, 5, 8 and 10 score the mean. He has also correctly perceived the direction of the deviations from the mean of the other subjects. However, he has made a mistake in his estimation of the size of the deviations, overestimating them all by two or three scale points. Cronbach calls this 'spread'. Once again the meaning of judge 2's different ratings is uncertain. It could represent a real difference in his opinion or it could represent only a different way of using the rating scale.

The third judge has a difference score of only 7 and is thus the most accurate judge, according to our test. Inspection of his data shows that he achieved his high accuracy in a very odd way. He does not differentiate the subjects at all, but gives everyone the mean score. The other two judges, although their ratings were not 'correct', had accurately perceived which subjects deviated from the mean, and in which direction. The third judge has not done so. Cronbach calls this an error in 'correlation'.

Obviously it is a very curious and very unsatisfactory scoring system that results in judge 3 getting a better accuracy score than judges 1 and 2. Any judge who correctly estimates the average score of the subjects is automatically at an advantage. Moreover, we saw in the discussion of empathy methods that there are good systematic reasons why it should be possible to estimate the average response. The subjects are often homogeneous, so they will tend to give similar responses, and they will be similar to the judge in many cases, so his assumption of similarity will be correct. Many traits are seen by judges and subjects as desirable or undesirable, so social desirability effects will also allow the judges to estimate the average response. All these effects can lead to high stereotype accuracy and a misleading estimate of the judge's ability to differentiate people.

In fact, Cronbach (1955) complicates matters considerably by considering the case of a difference score based on ratings of a number of subjects, on a number of traits. This produces seven components, instead of three. Since it is the author's contention that such global trait scores – over different subjects and different traits – are undesirable, the further four components will not be described.

There is some uncertainty about the status and significance of Cronbach's 'components' in trait-rating scores; we have been referring to them as artefacts and thereby implying that our only concern should be to eliminate them. This view is not taken by Cronbach, however, nor by many writers on the topic since. They regard the components not as artefacts, but as genuine and important aspects of the judgement process. Our aim should be to study them in their own right, rather than eliminate them. This is disputable however. Certainly Cronbach's observations are very valuable when we are considering judgement tasks that necessarily use numerical ratings, for example, school and university examinations, clinical ratings or supervisors' ratings in industry. On the other hand, if we are interested in the study of accuracy itself, we do not have to use ratings, if they present problems. We are using them only as a means to an end, and thus can substitute other methods. There are several possibilities.

(a) Refined difference scores. Cline and Crow have both developed ways of analysing difference scores that separate the various components. They still use global difference scores based on a number of subjects and a number of traits.

(b) Standard scores. If we analyse each trait separately – a desirable proceeding in any case – we can use standard scores and so eliminate individual differences in level and spread. Standard scores are, in fact, used for this purpose in some examination marking methods.

(c) Ranking. It would be possible to dispense with ratings altogether and use ranking (or sorting) methods. The judges would be forced to differentiate among the subjects and to do so in easily comparable ways.

Matching methods

This method has been used widely, particularly in studies that seek to establish that a particular judgement is possible, using a particular sample of behaviour. For example, it has been used to evaluate the usefulness of projective tests, like the Thematic Apperception Test (TAT) or Rorschach, in psychiatric diagnosis.

Judges and subjects. These are generally separate sets of people. Matching studies always use a number of subjects as this is essential to the method.

Sample of behaviour. In one version of the method, there is one sample of behaviour. In the other, there are two or more samples. The samples are very varied: handwriting, drawing, mosaics, photographs, biographical data or case histories, projective test data, etc.

Form and content of judgement. In the first form of the method the judge is given the set of samples of behaviour and instructed to match them to the appropriate subjects, that is, the subjects who produced them or to whom they belong. For example, Taft (1956) required his subjects to match forty mosaics to the forty subjects who produced them. In the second version of the test, the judge is given two more sets of samples of behaviour and instructed to sort into pairs or sets, each belonging to one subject. For example, Chambers and Hamlin (1957) find that psychiatrists can match Rorschach data to diagnostic labels, for a set of psychiatric patients, with a fair degree of accuracy.

Criterion. The criterion in matching experiments is very simple and entirely problem-free – the actual origin of the material.

Comments. The matching method involves no artefacts of the sort that beset other methods; there is no way the judge can 'cheat' and obtain an unrealistic score. The method also presents the judge with a sensible task which does not force him to make his judgements using concepts he would not normally use.

The method has one drawback: it yields only limited information. It tells us that a particular judgement is possible, given a particular set of information. Thus, it has been shown that projective test data, of various sorts, can be matched to particular patients or diagnostic categories with above chance accuracy (P. E. Vernon, 1964); but we do not know which particular item of information is used to make the judgement. This is a particular disadvantage where large samples of behaviour, such as case histories, are being used. Vernon suggests that often minor and trivial details – references to age or background – are used to make the judgement. However, the method is a useful first step, establishing that a particular judgement can be made; other methods can then be used to discover how the judgement is arrived at.

6 How Accurately we Judge

As we have seen, we are continually making judgements of various sorts about other people. Are we generally right in what we think about others or do we make mistakes? We saw in chapters 3 and 4 that there are systematic biases in most people's thinking about others, that are likely to lead to inaccurate judgements of others. We also saw in chapter 2 that some approaches to interpersonal perception – those that emphasize intuition – suggest that perception is always correct; the question of accuracy has, therefore, some theoretical interest.

Accuracy of perception is also a very important question from a practical point of view. A person who persistently fails to understand others will find life very difficult and unrewarding; indeed, some theories about mental illness consider that such a failure is central to the condition (Argyle, 1969). P. E. Vernon (1964) comments that accurate perception of others is important for the individual's self-esteem. One can admit to being a poor cricketer or to be shortsighted, but not to being socially imperceptive. Evidently accurate perception of others is an important matter, so it is essential to know how good people are at perceiving others and to be able to measure individual differences. It is also of considerable practical importance to have measures of accuracy for perfecting interviewing techniques, for clinical assessment and for improving perception in a wide variety of practical fields.

However, asking how good people are at judging others is rather like asking how large is a small social group: any verdict is relative. In the first place, accuracy is relative to the skill of the judges, so some care should be taken to obtain a reasonable sample of judges; most studies have used either students or professionals – psychiatrists, personnel managers, etc.

Inaccurate judgements occur because the judge's inference rules are incorrect or contain biases of the type discussed in chapters 3 and 4. Judgements may also be inaccurate because the task is too difficult or because the judge is not trying hard enough; these errors may be compared with errors in the perception of objects that are too far away to be seen properly or to which the judge is not attending. Similarly, we may misperceive others if we cannot see or hear them properly. This is particularly true of dynamic judgements, since these are made more quickly. In a crowded, noisy and poorly lit room, it is easy to misunderstand the other person. Errors can also arise if the judge is not attending closely or if he is too tired to absorb the information he receives. Inattention has almost certainly affected many experiments but has only been studied in one; Grossman (1963) finds that judges who watch stimulus films more closely perceive the subjects more accurately.

Accuracy is also relative to the skill or expressiveness of the subject; if he is very reserved or inexpressive, even the most perceptive judge will be poor at perceiving him. Many studies, especially those on the recognition of emotion, have used one subject only. There is evidence that some subjects are more easily or more accurately judged than others. Norsworthy (1910) finds that some girls in a group were judged more consistently than others. Tagiuri and Kogan (1957) find that some sociometric preferences are more visible than others. There are two possible reasons for this. Firstly, some people are not very expressive, as we have observed before. Secondly, as Goffman (1956) points out, people wish to present themselves in particular ways and this affects their behaviour; this 'self-presentation' could also obviously lead to erroneous impressions of what the subject is like.

A more serious problem concerns the nature of the judgement itself. In most studies the judge is provided with some information about the subject and asked to provide some further information. Obviously the information the judge is given must be sufficient to allow the judgement to be made at all but, on the other hand, should not be so extensive that he has only to use his memory to give the right answer. By using impossibly difficult or excessively easy tasks, it would be possible to 'prove' that judgements were all either very accurate or very inaccurate. Research on the accuracy of perception should use tasks that (a) are not too difficult and not too easy and that (b) discriminate between good and bad judges, giving a wide spread of individual differences.

In the rest of the chapter the literature on accuracy of judgements will be reviewed and each type of judgement discussed in turn, according to the classification put forward in chapter 1. The volume of research on each type of judgement varies considerably. Some types of judgement, for example, of the emotional expressions, have been studied extensively, whereas others have scarcely been studied at all.

Judgements of superficial characteristics

Relatively little work has been reported on the perception of superficial characteristics, possibly because there is little scope for error with many of them.

However some work has been reported on the identification of Jews by Jewish and non-Jewish judges. Early work produced conflicting and improbable results. For example, several studies reported that Jewish judges were unable to identify Jews at all, while other studies reported that anti-Semitic judges were good at doing so. These results were probably caused by two flaws in the design of the early studies. These experiments used free response methods, so that anti-Semitic judges could appear to be more accurate, by calling more of the subjects Jewish (although their accuracy of identification of non-Jewish subjects would be correspondingly reduced). Early studies also presented the task as the identification of Jews from photographs, so it is possible that Jews and non-prejudiced judges objected to the task because it implied Jews were physically different. Only the anti-Semitic judges took the task seriously. Toch, Rabin and Wilkins (1962) avoid the latter problem by disguising the task, and eliminate the other arte-fact by using a sorting procedure. They found that Jews were identified, whereas the judges could not distinguish be-tween Protestants and Catholics, and that Jewish judges were better at detecting Jews. Unfortunately, they did not study an anti-Semitic sample.

Most work on the perception of other races, of class, etc., has concentrated on stereotypes, rather than accuracy of perception. However, unpublished research by Mary Sissons has shown that social class can be identified quite accurately from photographs and from samples of recorded speech.

Rokeach (1945) reports that he did not find an assumed similarity effect when girls rated their own and other girls' attractiveness, since most girls rated themselves as more at-tractive than average. Assuming that Rokeach did not, in fact, have an above average sample, it follows that his sub-jects were poor at judging their own and possibly others' attractiveness. The literature on facial stereotypes has already been discussed in chapter 4.

Responses to particular situations and classes of situations

These two areas will be reviewed together, since they have generally been studied in the same experiments. The work on general personality traits (response to classes of situations) was done using the trait rating and empathy methods, and so is hard to interpret. Many studies find that traits can be rated and questionnaire responses predicted with above chance ac-curacy, but many of these studies may be measuring stereo-type accuracy rather than differential accuracy. Later studies by Cline and Richards (1960) and Crow and Hammond (1957) find that judges can judge accurately on a variety of tasks, including deciding which topics the subjects would refuse to discuss in public, which adjectives they would check as applying to themselves and how much they would score on scales such as 'paranoia', 'social contact', 'hypo-chondria', etc.

Since 1956 some research has been reported using Cline's set of filmed interviews and his tests, including the Behaviour Postdiction Test. These tests are relatively free from arte-facts and they also measure accuracy, for he has found that judges do consistently better than chance and also that there are individual differences that correlate with per-sonality. Cline (1964) also considers the question whether one person or a group is the better judge, a question of some practical importance. Cline compares individuals, face to face groups and 'statistical' groups, that is, the average esti-mate of several people. He finds that both kinds of group are better than individuals in general, but not better than the best individual judges. He suggests that the best way of ob-taining accurate judgements, therefore, is to take the average of several judges, rather than waste time allowing a group to discuss the issue or trying to identify the best judges.

A number of studies have been reported on the judgement of intelligence from photos, with inconclusive results. This is a rather pointless type of experiment, however, since no one would normally base judgements on such unlikely evidence. Little systematic work has been reported since, despite the obvious interest of the question. A few findings have emerged incidentally. Crow and Hammond (1957) report that their judges could judge vocabulary scores of their sub-jects, as measured by the Wechsler Intelligence Test.

Work on specific abilities for particular occupations is dis-cussed in chapter 8.

Relatively little work has been reported on the perception of attitudes as such, possibly because we have little difficulty finding out what others think about particular issues. Some empathy studies have used questionnaires concerning 'values', for example, the Kuder Inventory which dis-tinguishes people who value 'artistic' careers from people who value sales careers; these studies have found some accuracy of perception. However, it might be worth studying the perception of more basic dimensions of attitudes, such as authoritarianism; several studies have examined the perception of other attributes by judges who differ in authoritarianism, but none have studied the perception of authoritarianism itself.

Sociometric judgements

Some work has been reported on the perception of liking and disliking. Tagiuri (1958) reports that people can say who in a group likes them with a better than chance accuracy, but admits that the assumed liking problem makes this finding hard to interpret. He also reports that people are much less accurate at guessing who dislikes them and suggests various explanations for this, for example, that people show dislike less plainly than like. However, the more parsimonious explanation is that this is an assumed liking effect. If we assume people like us, we will be incorrect if, in fact, they do not like us – hence the apparent inability to perceive dislike.

Tagiuri also reports that people are good at judging who likes who in the group, as opposed to who likes them. There is no reason to expect an assumed liking effect if the judge is not involved in the comparison, so this may represent a genuine finding. Crow and Hammond report above chance accuracy on a variety of sociometric tasks involving judgements of leadership, cooperation and likeability, but do not describe their results in detail.

Affective judgements

There is a large literature on the recognition of emotions, and a number of findings have emerged. Early studies underestimated the judge's ability to identify the emotions portrayed, partly because they counted the judge's response as wrong, unless the judge used the precise word the experimenter had in mind. Thus if the judge said 'contempt', when the experimenter intended the photograph to portray 'disgust', the judge was considered to be wrong. Woodworth (1938) re-analyses previous data and finds that the various emotions can be grouped into six categories so that errors in identification are rarely more than one step away from the correct answer. His six categories are as follows:

1. Love, happiness, mirth
2. Surprise
3. Fear, suffering
4. Anger, determination
5. Disgust
6. Contempt

Schlosberg (1954) finds the ends of the scale can be joined up to form a circle, and Woodworth's finding about the distance of errors still holds. Further work by Schlosberg and others finds that two or possibly three dimensions – pleasant-ness–unpleasantness, attention–rejection and (possibly) level of activation – can be used to describe facial expressions.

A few studies have reported that some emotions are more easily identifiable than others. For example, studies using the Feleky pictures find that fear, horror and surprise were more easily identified than other emotions. However, no con-clusion can be drawn from this, for it could be that Feleky expressed fear, horror and surprise better than other emotions. Only studies using a number of subjects can con-tribute anything to this question. Thompson and Meltzer (1964) use a large number of subjects and find that hap-piness, love, fear and determination are identified more ac-curately than disgust, contempt and suffering. The finding that 'love' was more easily identified is rather surprising. Thompson and Meltzer conclude that their subjects may have been identifying the embarrassment produced in their subjects when asked to portray love. Davitz (1964), studying vocal expression of emotion, finds that subjectively similar emotions, for example, joy and cheerfulness, are more diffi-cult to discriminate than dissimilar emotions; this finding is implied by Woodworth's six category system.

A number of studies have tried to identify the particular facial cues associated with various emotions. Darwin (1872) suggests that facial expressions evolve from the organism's responses to particular situations; this theory implies that there should be consistent facial patterns specific to particular situations. For some reason early work concentrated on trying to discover whether particular emotions were better expressed by the lower or upper half of the face. The results of these studies were inconclusive, not surprisingly since most of them used only one subject. Landis (1929) examines the involvement of particular muscle groups in a number of subjects. He finds little specificity, except for the startle response, but this may have been caused by the operation of 'display rules'. Davitz (1964) suggests that facial movement may be related to Schlosberg's dimensions rather than to specific emotions; this is an interesting suggestion, worth looking into.

Some work on the vocal expression of emotion has been reported by Pollack, Rubinstein and Horowitz (1960) who find that emotions can still be identified through a considerable amount of noise, showing that there is some redundancy in emotional expression. This in turn implies that identification of emotions, etc., in actual encounters will be easier and more certain, since the judge will have a larger sample to judge from.

In most studies the expression is presented without any context. Langfeld (1918) finds that suggestions made to the judges by the experimenter are readily accepted by them showing that it is possible to read into the photographs a variety of meanings. Frijda (1958) shows that giving the photographs a context affects judgements of them considerably, and goes on to suggest that the expression alone gives only very basic information about the person's mood, for example, that he is displeased, and that knowledge of the context is required to distinguish between disgust and anger, for example.

The results of studies using photographs taken from life show, according to Tagiuri (1969), generally inferior accuracy compared with those studies that use posed photographs, partly because subjects in live photographs often produce unexpected expressions. For example, many of

Landis's subjects smiled when they saw a rat decapitated. This does not mean that Landis's subjects were pleased or happy; rather it points to an interesting feature of expression of emotion. People do not always allow their feelings to show but often put on a front or 'self-presentation'. Ekman and Friesen (1969) suggest that there are 'display rules' for facial expression, that determine whether an expression will be made openly, or modified, or suppressed altogether. Lazarus (1969) finds evidence of the operation of these rules in a study using Japanese and American subjects. The subjects watched an unpleasant film alone and showed many facial expressions of disgust, etc. However, when questioned about the film by the experimenter, the Japanese showed no signs of disgust but remained impassive; the American subjects, on the other hand, showed the same expressions as when they had seen the film alone. The results of this study make Landis's apparently bizarre results more intelligible.

Relatively few studies have been reported on the perception of states other than those in the 'Schlosberg circle'. Argyle and Williams (1969) find that people are surprisingly bad at estimating the proportion of time another person looks at them. Jecker, Maccoby and Breitrose (1965) have developed a method of studying how good teachers are at recognizing when a child has understood something. Another source of information comes from 'verbal conditioning' studies (Krasner, 1958). In these studies the subject responds to a variety of signs of approval and disapproval given by the experimenter. He has, in effect, responded to cues emitted by the experimenter; there is some controversy about whether he does so consciously or not.

7 The Good Judge of Others

This chapter will be divided into three sections. In the first section, the generality of accuracy in judgement across different situations will be reviewed. In the second, the literature on individual differences in ability will be discussed, together with the work on personality correlates. In the third section, work on improving ability to judge by training will be discussed.

The generality of the ability to judge others

The first question is whether the ability to judge others is general or not; does accuracy in the recognition of emotions from photographs also imply that the judge will be accurate in completing an inventory, for example? If ability is not general the literature on individual differences will have to be discussed for each type of judgement separately. There are a number of ways in which ability to judge others might be general: across tasks, across attributes, across subjects and over time.

Generality across tasks

As we saw in chapter 5, there are a variety of different methods of testing accuracy, that present the judge with different judgement tasks. Several large-scale studies using a variety of tasks have been reported. Studies done before 1955 are generally discounted because they may have contained artefacts; it is worth noting, however, that artefacts of the type discussed in chapter 5 would produce spurious positive relationships, whereas the studies of generality of ability before 1955 report predominantly negative results, which could not be produced by artefacts.

P. E. Vernon (1933) finds very few correlations between a large number of tests, although there is slight evidence of correlations within four groups of tests: accuracy of predicting ratings of self by others, accuracy of ratings of others, accuracy of perception of strangers (which includes recognition of emotion tasks), and a set of tests, of doubtful validity, involving writing character sketches; Vernon found no evidence for generality of ability across tasks and little evidence of generality within tasks. Wedeck (1947) finds that various tests of identifying emotions and personality from photographs correlate together, but do not correlate with a test of ability to detect lies produced by an actor before the judges. Taft (1956) finds a small correlation between ability to estimate group responses to the Minnesota Multiphasic Personality Inventory (MMPI) and a trait-rating task. The latter uses a global difference score, so is possibly a measure of stereotype accuracy; this would account for its correlation with the group test. Neither test correlated with a test of matching mosaics with their authors.

Two more recent studies that controlled for artefacts have been reported more recently, and produce conflicting results. Crow and Hammond (1957) gave their subjects fifteen tests, divided into three groups. In the first the judges saw films of the subjects and judged the subjects on a reticence test – what topics the subjects would refuse to discuss, on a vocabulary test and on a global trait-rating test. The results were analysed by the Random Comparison Method, devised by Crow to avoid artefacts. The second group was a series of sociometric tests of leadership, cooperation and liking, and the third was a group opinion test. None of the tests correlated together. Only six of a possible 105 correlations were significant, and these were all small. Even tests that might be expected to correlate, such as the various sociometric tests, did not. On the other hand Cline and Richards (1960) find high correlations between various tests – Behaviour Postdiction Test, sentence completion, opinion prediction, adjective check list and trait rating – that his judges took after seeing films of the subjects. Cline and Richards analysed the trait ratings into stereotype and differential accuracy and found that each correlated with the other tests, although the correlations with stereotype accuracy were generally higher. Cline and Richards suggest that some judges were accurate overall because they distinguished accurately between different subjects (differential accuracy), others because they estimated the average score (stereotype accuracy) and some because they did both. Bronfenbrenner, Harding and Gallway (1958) reach similar conclusions. Cline and Richards suggest that accuracy of judgement is a general trait but, like intelligence, has 'group factors', that is, certain groups of tests correlate together more highly than others, but all tests correlate positively. However, this conclusion is not justified, since Cline and Richards's study is the only one to report large correlations between different tests and because their results differ so much from those of Crow and Hammond. More research is required to determine whether judging ability is general or, if not, what types of ability are separate from each other, or whether Cline and Richards are right in supposing judging ability to have a hierarchical structure, like intelligence.

Generality across particular attributes

Some studies combine the data from a number of scales to give a global index accuracy. Others examine each trait separately, so that it is possible to determine whether the judges can judge, for example, extraversion as accurately as intelligence. It is possible that people who regularly make a particular type of judgement – for example, of intelligence – become highly skilled at this particular judgement, without any 'transfer' to judgements of other attributes. Some studies also examine the judge's ability to judge the same trait, but use two different criteria. For example, Crow and Hammond (1957) test their judge's ability to perceive the 'apparent' and 'real' possession of various traits. In the former case, the subjects' self-ratings are the criterion, while in the latter, the subject's personality inventory scores are used. Those studies that examine the accuracy of judgement of each trait or attribute, in a particular judgement task, generally find positive correlations, often on the low side. Where the traits are measured by subscales of the same inventory, higher correlations have been found: Gage (1952) finds correlations of 0·50 between subscales of the Kuder Inventory of Personal Values. (These findings may be an artefact. Gage concludes that his judges were using stereotypes. If a judge had the correct stereotype and if the subscales of the inventory were related, the judge need, in effect, make only one judgement – identify the stereotype. It follows that his scores for the subscales would be related. A convincing demonstration of generality across traits should use scales that are not correlated.)

Studies of the identification of emotions have found that ability to judge is consistent across the various emotions, although the accuracy with which each is identified varies from study to study. Levy (1964) reports that ability to identify emotions presented facially correlates with ability to identify the same emotions presented vocally.

Generality across subjects

Most studies, except those on recognition of emotion, use more than one subject person, so we can determine whether ability to judge one person accurately implies the ability to judge another person accurately, or all people accurately. The ability to judge others may be general across all individuals or it may be specific to certain classes, for example, people of the same sex, age, etc.

A number of early studies reported generality across subjects, but these studies used unrefined measures that may have measured stereotype accuracy. If the judges were using stereotypes and if the subjects were similar, the judge would be consistently accurate for different subjects. Bronfenbrenner, Harding and Gallway (1958) using refined measures, find no consistency at all across subjects, taken overall, but do find some more complex relationships, to be discussed in a later section.

Taft (1955) concludes that judges are better at judging

those of the same sex, age and background as themselves, which may mean only that their stereotypes or assumptions of similarity are correct for these subjects and not for others. Bronfenbrenner, Harding and Gallway (1958) find evidence of complex relationships between sex of judge and sex of subjects, when people in groups rated each other. Male judges were consistent across the two sexes, that is, those good at judging men were also good at judging women, but women were not. The better a woman was at judging her own sex, the worse she was at judging men. This accounts for Bronfenbrenner and colleagues' failure to find a general consistency across subjects, regardless of sex, and implies that future work should always examine sex differences.

Several studies have been reported on the relative accuracy of judgement of friends and strangers. Travers (1943) finds that judges who can estimate the proportion of their group who know a particular word, can also estimate accurately the proportion of the American population who know it. Taft (1966) finds that the accuracy of judging a single friend does not correlate at all with the accuracy of judging a single stranger, although the assumption of similarity between the two did correlate quite well.

A number of studies consider insight or self-awareness, that is, the correlation between the judge's ability to perceive himself accurately and his ability to perceive others accurately. There are problems involved in measuring insight, however. The usual criterion is the rating of the judge by a number of other people. This is unsatisfactory since many studies have shown that such ratings are often inaccurate. It has also been found that some people are harder to judge than others, so that ratings by others would be an unreliable criterion. Social desirability can also affect the ratings. Subjects in psychological experiments usually present themselves favourably on ratings and inventories; they also tend not to be very critical of the people they are judging, so most of the ratings will be favourable. This can give rise to the interesting but spurious finding that people with 'good' personalities also have good insight. Taft (1955) concludes that several studies have found a correlation between insight and ability to judge others. Some of these studies found a correlation when undesirable traits were studied, so their results cannot be attributed to social desirability effect. The question of insight was also discussed in chapter 3, page 54.

Generality over time

If a test of accuracy of judgement does not produce consistent results on different occasions, we would assume that it is unreliable, although it is conceivable the subject's personality has changed in the meantime.

Early studies all report a fair degree of consistency over time, indicating that their tests of accuracy are measuring something. Unfortunately it is not always certain that early studies measure differential accuracy, rather than stereotype accuracy or the subject's response biases on rating scales. Crow and Hammond report reasonable test–retest reliabilities for stereotype accuracy, but not for differential accuracy scores.

Conclusion

The work on generality of judging ability is somewhat inconclusive. Early studies are hard to interpret, and later studies, using more adequate measures, give conflicting results. Interest in the problem has faded for no good reason and no further research has been reported. Many questions remain unanswered, for example, the relation between ability to judge personality traits or predict specific behaviour, and the recognition of emotions, or the relations of these two abilities with perception of sociometric choice. The best conclusion to draw is that work in this important area ought to be continued.

Individual differences in ability

Since it is uncertain whether ability is general or not, the next section will discuss the relationship between individual differences and specific tests of accuracy.

Age

Judgements of sociometric choice and recognition of facial and vocal expression of emotions improve as children grow older. No studies have been reported on accuracy of other types of judgement in children of different ages, although there is extensive literature on development of children's concepts of other people and on the different cues used at different ages, which has been mentioned in earlier chapters.

Sex

It has often been stated that women show a slight but consistent superiority in recognition of emotion and in judgements of personality, but in fact the evidence is so conflicting that this conclusion is not justified. For example, Taft (1955) reports that, of nine studies of emotion recognition, three found a slight superiority for women, one a slight superiority for man and five found no difference between the sexes. The literature could be more accurately summarized by saying that sex differences, when they occur, more usually favour women, but that they do not usually occur. However, there is evidence that women attend to different cues and form different types of judgements (see pages 46 and 49). One finding may be mentioned: Witryol and Kaess (1957) find that women (college students) are definitely better at 'social memory' – remembering people's names – than men.

Demographic variables

A number of studies of family size, social class, race, etc. have been reported and will be described together, since it is often hard to identify the key variable. Thus Taft (1955) reports that children in rural areas were less accurate on a trait-rating task and that Negroes and foreigners (in the US) were less accurate, while Jews were more accurate. However, he also reports that only children and children from smaller families were more accurate – possibly because they had more contact with adults in childhood. This family size effect could account for some of the other relationships mentioned above, assuming that people in rural areas or Negroes have large families. Similarly, the finding of a positive relationship between class and accuracy in predicting group responses is probably accounted for by class differences in intelligence.

Intelligence

Intelligence has been found to correlate with a wide variety of judgement tasks: trait rating, recognition of emotion, empathy and judgement of strangers. The correlations are not always very large, possibly because many studies used college students for subjects, giving a small spread of intelligence. It is also important to note that none of the studies reporting correlations use refined measures of accuracy, so they could all be measuring primarily stereotype accuracy. Sechrest and Jackson (1961) find no relation between differential accuracy and academic achievement or intelligence as rated by peers, nor do they find any relation between intelligence and stereotype accuracy. Unfortunately, they do not use actual intelligence scores as a criterion.

Cognitive complexity

Bieri (1955) finds that judges who have many concepts for describing others, that is, who are 'cognitively complex' (see page 49) are more accurate and assume less similarity: the latter finding has been replicated, but not the former.

Social skill and popularity

It is often thought that a person who perceives others accurately will be socially effective and more popular; Steiner (1955) points out that accuracy of perception may not improve social relations, unless the right things are perceived. A person who always perceives others' shortcomings accurately or who perceives that others dislike him might well find this a hindrance to social contact. The ability to perceive roles and group opinion, on the other hand, might be very useful.

There are problems in measuring popularity or social skill. Early workers used tests of 'social intelligence' that were no more than tests of verbal intelligence. Other work uses sociometric criteria which have greater validity, but which often have assumed liking problems (as described on pages 54 and 89). This artefact could be avoided by using ranking or forced choice methods. Other studies use criterion groups – people who are presumed to be high on social skill, such as salesmen, leaders, psychiatrists. However, this presumption is sometimes incorrect; for example, psychiatrists are no better than average at perceiving others. It is also not clear that the same type of skill is involved in every case.

Several studies find that ability to judge group opinion correlates with popularity and efficiency in work situations. Taft (1956) finds that good judges of others are less 'ingenious' in a role playing situation and do not differ from others in rated persuasiveness or popularity. No more recent studies have been done using refined measures of accuracy and more satisfactory criteria of popularity and social skill. Hornstein (1967) finds that compatibility between room mates is related to their ability to perceive each other's vocal expressions of emotions. Levy (1964) finds that accuracy of recognition of vocal emotional expression is correlated with the judge's ability to express the same emotion.

Personality attributes

Several early studies report that judges who are maladjusted, by various criteria, are less accurate at rating traits. Several studies using the MMPI, both as criterion of adjustment and, in some cases, as judging instrument, find similar relationships. One study reports a positive relation between adjustment and ability to recognize emotions facially.

Several recent studies examine the personality of accurate judges, using refined measures of accuracy and variety of personality attributes; the results of these studies are complex but point the same way. Two studies, Dymond (1950) and Taft (1955), report that good judges are more sociable, although Taft also suggests that detachment in social relations is characteristic of accurate judges. Grossman (1963) finds differential accuracy related to tough-mindedness and a tendency to be empirical and nonconforming. The literature of personality correlates of accuracy has some curious omissions: for example, no systematic work has been reported using basic dimensions like extraversion or neuroticism. Sechrest and Jackson (1961) find no correlation between differential accuracy and a variety of measures: MMPI scales, sociometric ratings, repertory grid and Rorschach scores, etc. They do find correlations between stereotype accuracy and sociometric ratings of pleasantness and predictability, and absence of psychopathic deviance on the MMPI. Chance and Meaders (1960) find that judges with good differential accuracy show a pattern of self-ratings of independence, strong-mindedness, participation in social relations and absence of introspection.

Bronfenbrenner, Harding and Gallway (1958) find that sex of judge and sex of subject is related to personality characteristics of good judges, which could account for the inconclusive results of other research that did not consider sex differences. The following pattern was found:

Table 2
Personality Characteristics of Good Judges

	of male subjects	of female subjects
Male judges	resourceful dominant outgoing not very tactful	tactful tolerant timid
Female judges	submissive reasonable accepting	submissive insecure inhibited unattractive

If the personality of good male judges is examined without considering sex of subject, the contrasting descriptions cancel each other out and no correlations are found. The results are reasonably similar to those of Chance and Meaders, who use only male subjects and judges and find good judges are high on affiliation and dominance and not very reflective. Grossman also uses only males; his results are reasonably similar. Bronfenbrenner, Harding and Gallway also consider stereotype accuracy and conclude that the good judge of stereotypes tends himself to fit American middle-class ideal stereotypes; the men are seen as outgoing, self-assured, uninhibited and rather objectionable, while the women are controlled, well socialized and competent. The latter result is similar to Sechrest and Jackson's findings.

The results of these studies are interesting. Bronfenbrenner and colleagues' data suggest that other studies fail to find any significant relationships because they do not take account of sex differences. There is also an encouraging similarity between the Bronfenbrenner findings about male judges of male subjects, and Chance and Meaders's data, and between Sechrest and Jackson and Bronfenbrenner and colleagues about women judges with stereotype accuracy, even though different judgements tasks and different personality measures are used. However, the picture of the good male judge that emerges is rather unexpected. The good male judge of males is described as a rather insensitive aggressive person while the good male judge of females is described as very ineffectual. The good female judges are described slightly more favourably. The results suggest that Steiner (1955) is right and that the good judge of others might not be socially polished and confident. Bronfenbrenner and colleagues point out that they were dealing with first impressions; a different picture might emerge in an established relationship.

Mental and character disorders

Some work has been reported on the accuracy of perception of others by various abnormal groups.

Most work has been done with schizophrenic patients. It has been discovered that schizophrenics are quite unable to recognize emotions conveyed by tone of voice, or facial expression or stick figures, although they respond to verbal expressions of emotion and interpersonal attitudes, Milgram (1960) reports that schizophrenics cannot predict word associations given by male and female subjects. It has also been shown that their synchronizing – timing their utterances – is very bad (Matarazzo and Saslow, 1961). More generally it has been observed in numerous studies (see Argyle, 1969) that their social behaviour is grossly abnormal; they do not orient towards others, do not look at them and do not produce appropriate replies to anything said to them. The question arises whether they fail to perceive others or to interact normally because they cannot or because they do not want to. It has been suggested that schizophrenics are over-aroused and avoid social contact because it makes their over-arousal worse. Argyle (1969), on the other hand, suggests that the failure to perceive or interact may be a failure of the central translation process that translates perception into response.

Some patients are diagnosed as 'paranoid' and such patients, almost by definition, perceive others very inaccurately. The typical paranoid patient sees everything and everyone as a threat to him and imagines plots against him that do not exist.

Some research has been reported on the perception of psychopaths. Gough and Petersen (1952) constructed a test for detecting psychopathic patients, based on the assumption that they do not perceive other people's feelings and do not predict their behaviour accurately; this test distinguishes psychopathic patients from normals. Gough (1948) reports that as a consequence of the psychopath's inability to understand other people's reactions, he does not understand punishment and disapproval. It has been suggested that some psychopaths can understand others' behaviour but ignore others' feelings, because they manipulate people like objects; however, there is little evidence that this is true.

There is less systematic evidence about other types of mental illness. It seems likely that many neurotics do not pay enough attention to the thoughts and feelings of others, although there is no research on the ability of neurotics to perceive emotions or more enduring aspects of others accurately.

Conclusion

Some interesting results emerge, although much more work is still required. It has been shown that intelligence is related to ability on a variety of judgement tasks, although Sechrest and Jackson (1961) fail to find a correlation using a refined measure of accuracy. The work on social skill and popularity is less satisfactory, and recent results suggest that accurate judges may not be highly confident and skilled in social contacts. The literature on perception by those with mental or character disorders suggests that perception is generally very defective although it is not clear whether they are unable or unwilling to form accurate judgements. The literature on the good judge of others is interesting and suggestive rather than conclusive; many issues need to be settled by further research.

Improvement of accuracy of interpersonal perception by training

Relatively little worthwhile research on the usefulness of training has been reported, probably because of the difficulty of measuring accuracy. A number of studies have reported improved accuracy, but have used inadequate criteria. Some studies have used ratings by others as the criterion of improvement in a person's accuracy as a result of training; this is obviously unsatisfactory.

Two studies (Davitz, 1964; Guilford, 1929) show that the accuracy of identification of emotions by face and voice can be improved by giving the judges the 'correct' answers during a practice session; Jecker, Maccoby and Breitrose (1965) similarly find that 'knowledge of results' or 'feedback' improved teachers' perception of pupils' comprehension. On the other hand Crow (1957) finds that clinical training does not improve the accuracy of trainee psychiatrists' perception on trait-rating tasks. The trainees differentiated among the subjects more, but these differentiations did not match the criterion scores, so overall accuracy actually declined. The content of the clinical training was not specified.

Recent research concentrates on trying to improve the whole social performance of the individual, not just his perception. Role playing and 'T (or training) groups' have been used. (See Argyle, 1969, for a discussion of these methods.) Some of these studies specifically look at accuracy of perception and find that people who have been in T groups do not improve their performance on trait-rating tasks. However, it is found that they make greater use of 'psychological' terms and concepts which can give them and others the impression that they have improved their perceptiveness.

The literature on training is so small that it is hard to draw any very definite conclusions. It does seem, however, that studies that have used specific procedures, for example, knowledge of results, have produced a positive improvement, whereas those that have relied only on unsystematic methods, like clinical training or T groups, have not.

8 Practical Applications

Many judgements of others are made informally, during everyday encounters. Such judgements are made relatively casually and, in many cases, it does not much matter if they are inaccurate. (Indeed it is often slightly misleading to call them judgements: 'impression' would be a more appropriate term.) Other judgements are made very formally, however, fully deserving the name 'judgement', and these are often very important. It matters to an organization to select people who will be able to do their jobs properly. It is important that the psychiatrist should be able to say what is wrong with his patient and even more important that he should select the right form of treatment. Nor are psychiatrists the only professionals who try to diagnose and treat other people's problems. Child guidance, student 'counselling', vocational guidance, probation work all involve the accurate perception of important basic features. There are many other instances of 'professional' judgements. Teachers observe their pupils and form impressions of their abilities and behaviour. Police and lawyers, and sometimes laymen, form judgements about a suspect's honesty. Staff in shops, hotels, etc., form opinions about the customer's needs and credit-worthiness. The mass media – press and broadcasting – send reporters out to observe important events and report on what has happened and what it means. In all these examples professional people perceive and form judgements about people and events. Are these judgements correct? And if not, why are they incorrect and what can be done to improve them?

This chapter will be divided into two sections. The first will deal with selection. A vast amount of research has been reported on selection, in a great variety of situations, using many different methods. The second section will deal with psychiatric diagnosis and similar assessments in social work, vocational guidance, 'counselling', etc. The psychiatrist or social worker has two aims: to decide what the subject's problem is and to solve it or help to solve it.

Selection

Whenever someone applies for a job of almost any sort, or whenever someone wants to enter higher education or specialized training of any sort, and often when someone seeks promotion or upgrading, his suitability will be assessed in one way or another. There is scarcely any job that does not have some sort of requirement, if only a 'negative' requirement like absence of criminal record. The better the job, the more extensive the requirements are. Furthermore, for many jobs and for most forms of higher education and special training the number who would like to be allowed to do them exceeds the number that can be taken, so it becomes necessary to try to select the best applicants. Most people go through a number of selection procedures at various times in their lives. The first comes usually at the age of eleven when some children are selected for grammar school. The next major selection comes when they leave school and try to get a job of some sort or try to get into higher education. These processes of selection can determine the direction of the person's life, so it is important to be certain that they are done as accurately as possible; the study of selection has become one of the most important areas of applied psychology.

This section will first consider briefly the history of work on selection and then describe some of the methods now used. Then the important questions of reliability and validity will be considered, and the usefulness of various methods will be discussed. Finally some tentative suggestions for improvement of the interview will be made.

History

The scientific study of selection has a relatively short history, possibly because selection by supposed merit is itself a recent invention. In primitive societies very little selection is needed, since there is little or no differentiation of social roles. More complex societies have social structures involving better jobs and opportunities but little selection takes place, since the class system prevents most of the population being considered. However, the spread of education and the increasing complexity of industrial societies makes selection by merit more and more desirable. Thus in the last century, the British Civil Service was reformed and jobs were given by examination, not by patronage and nepotism. Often sheer weight of numbers made systematic assessment necessary. In both world wars, millions of new soldiers were enlisted and had to be evaluated; and thousands of new officers were needed who could not be selected by the traditional method of personal acquaintance and social background. In the First World War all American recruits had their intelligence tested, the first example of large-scale scientific assessment. Between the wars, a great deal of work was done on assessment, mostly in the US. However, the new German Army also developed psychological testing methods for selecting officers, although they did not attempt to determine their validity. The Second World War saw the adoption of similar methods in both the US and Britain. In Britain, the three services devised elaborate methods of selection for both specialized 'trades' like radio mechanics, and for officer selection. In the army, all recruits were screened and their intelligence, aptitudes and stability assessed, before they were allocated to different units, and the War Office Selection Board (WOSB) was devised to select officers. More important, some attempt was made to ensure that the methods used were valid, that is, actually did select the right man for the job. Since the Second World War selection has been well established in Britain, although not to the same extent as in the US. Nevertheless, many of the methods used are invalid or have never been tested properly.

Methods

There are innumerable methods for determining an applicant's suitability for a job or special training, but they may be divided into four general categories: interviews, references and testimonials, biographical data and tests given by the assessors.

The interview. The interview is a well-established procedure used for almost every job and in many other circumstances; it has recently been reported that 99 per cent of people who are employed in any capacity in the US are first interviewed.

Interviews vary in a number of ways:

1. There may be one interviewer or a number.

2. The length of the interview can vary from a few minutes to over an hour. In some procedures the candidate is interviewed several times.

3. The interviewer's manner can vary. Some are friendly and try to put the candidate at his ease, while others are more aggressive or more formal.

4. The interviewer may already have other information about the candidate – references, qualifications, test results, etc., or may not.

5. The interviewer can look for a great variety of information and may or may not know in advance what information he is going to seek. Some interviewers use a written list of questions to be asked or facts to be elicited. The information the interviewer looks for may be of four general types.

(a) He can ask for straightforward information about, for example, typing skill, age, education, etc., and can clarify points from an application form that are not clear, for example, what arrangements a working mother will make for her children, what pay the applicant wants for the job. (b) He can evaluate superficial aspects of the applicant's dress, appearance, etc. These are sometimes relevant although it seems probable that too much emphasis is placed on such things in most circumstances.

The types of information mentioned so far involve little in the way of judgement or inference; the following two types of information the interviewer may seek are less superficial.

(c) The interviewer often has to assess the candidate's suitability for the job, and decide which of several suitable applicants is the best. The definition of a suitable candidate will, of course, vary according to the job; an applicant for a research post will require such characteristics as originality and a good knowledge of his area, whereas a fireman might require courage and a degree of physical strength.

(d) The interviewer may also try to evaluate the candidate's personality in relation to the job, and this might include forming judgements of stability, perseverance, sociability, etc.

Obviously it is not possible to list all the possible judgements that might be made, since these differ according to the job. The interviewer, and those engaged in selecting applicants, often have to decide the characteristics required for the job: this is called 'job evaluation' and can be a highly complex and specialized skill in itself.

The way in which the interviewer forms his judgement can vary. He can reach a single overall or 'global' judgement about the candidate's suitability or he can form separate opinions about a number of attributes and base his final verdict on these. Both methods have pitfalls. In the former, the interviewer may not know why he selects the candidate and may, in fact, be ignoring some useful information or even basing his judgement entirely on useless and irrelevant information. In the latter, there is a likelihood of 'halo effects', so that only one judgement is actually made, but it is stated in a number of supposedly independent ways. Furthermore, the interviewer may not know what weight to assign to various items of information, especially where he has references, test data, etc., to consider as well. In a large organization, where a lot of people are selected for the same job, it may be possible to develop statistical or 'actuarial' weightings for various items of information so that the importance of each is known; this would not, however, be worthwhile unless the particular vacancy has to be filled very frequently.

References and testimonials. References are very widely used for almost all jobs and often for other purposes, for example, in selecting a tenant for a house. Most references given in Britain are free descriptions. The people asking for the reference do not ask for specific information and the people giving it do not usually present the data in a systematic way. It is possible, therefore, that useful information is omitted by accident. Also, it should be noted that the reference represents someone's opinion or judgement of the candidate and so is open to the usual biases. Obviously the candidate will give, as reference, someone he expects to give a favourable description. On the other hand, the person giving the reference may have seen far more of the candidate than the people doing the selecting and so his judgement may be far more useful. References are often useful as a quick, cheap way of 'screening' a lot of candidates and drawing up a 'short-list' of people to be interviewed or examined at greater length.

Biographical data and previous achievements. For most jobs the candidate is required to give information about his age, education, qualifications, experience, etc. This information can sometimes be very useful; for example, a person who has changed his job six times in as many years may well do so again. A man with ten years' driving experience and a 'clean' licence would probably be suitable for a job including driving. Such background information is often in-

cluded in 'actuarial' predictions, where its significance can be
properly evaluated.

Tests given by the selection team. These fall into three categories: general ability, specific aptitude and personality.
There is not usually any need to measure general intelligence
or ability, since academic qualifications are generally a good
index of this. However, many US universities use a special
intelligence test for selecting graduate students and senior
civil servants in Britain are also tested in this way. Tests of
special aptitude are, of course, very varied. Most involve an
approximation of the job itself, for example, sending Morse
code for a wireless operator. Tests of this type have been
used extensively in selection of army officers, both in Britain
and the US. The candidate is put in charge of a group of
other candidates and his skill in leading and organizing the
group is rated by observers. In one American test the candidate directs two 'helpers' who are actually confederates of
the assessment staff, and who act in different unhelpful ways,
one enthusiastic but clumsy and the other disagreeable and
uncooperative. (This method proved to have little validity
however.) Group discussions and lectures by candidates are
also used. Yet another variation is the 'in-basket test', where
the candidate has to deal with various paper work represen-
tative of the job. Situational tests often do not give objective
scores, but only observers' ratings.

Personality tests are extensively used in the US, but not
to any great extent in Britain

Reliability and validity. The aim of selection is to select the
right man for the job or the best applicants for specialized
training, so it follows that questions of accuracy or correctness of choice are very important. Does the selection
procedure pick out a man who does the job well? Are the
people who are selected for specialized training those most
likely to benefit from it? Many naïve observers and,
indeed, many professional selectors assume that selection is
always completely effective. Unfortunately, this is often far

from true. Studies of the reliability and validity of interviews and other selection methods commonly produce very depressing results.

To say that a test or measure is reliable means that it gives consistent results, that is, it does measure something. Most physical measurements are perfectly reliable: if a piece of wood is measured with a ruler ten times, the ten measurements will usually be identical. However, most psychological measurements are not perfectly reliable; that is, the successive measurements of someone's intelligence or extraversion will not give identical scores. Many tests are completely unreliable, so that successive measurements with them give completely unrelated scores. The reliability of the interview can be assessed in two ways: inter-interviewer reliability and test–retest reliability. The same method can be used for objective tests although it may be necessary to use parallel forms of the test. If the interview is reliable, then two interviewers should agree about the candidate, and the same interviewer, seeing the candidate for a second time, should reach the same verdict as on the first occasion.

Determining the validity of the interview is a more complicated problem. It requires a good criterion of the candidate's subsequent success or failure, of whether he 'really' is the right man for the job. Two types of criterion have been used in selection research – ratings and objective criteria. The rating method has been very widely used. After the candidate has been in the job for some time, his suitability is assessed by his superiors, usually on several relevant dimensions. For example, P. E. Vernon (1950), in a follow-up study of selection procedures for the administrative grade of the civil service, uses superiors' ratings of the candidates. The rating method is not very satisfactory from a theoretical point of view. The superiors' ratings are themselves judgements, so the question of validity can again be raised. What guarantee is there that these ratings are 'correct' and really measure the candidate's efficiency?

To try to validate the ratings could involve recourse to ratings of the superiors, but then these may be invalid; there is a danger of an infinite regress of ratings. On the other hand, it can be argued that efficiency by definition means making a favourable impression on one's superiors, so the rating method must be valid. There is some force in this argument, although it would fall down if the superior were manifestly inefficient, biased or had an incorrect or outdated view of the job.

There are numerous objective criteria of efficiency or suitability, varying according to the circumstances. For example, efficiency of selection for school and university is often assessed by examination marks or degree classes. Efficiency in industry can be assessed by productivity, absenteeism, turnover, etc. It is often difficult to find a suitable objective criterion for many jobs, etc., where there is no clearly defined end product. The objective criterion method appears to have advantages, but on closer scrutiny has a number of snags. The criterion is often not really objective; for example, exam marks, in Britain at any rate, depend on the subjective judgement of the examiner. Other genuinely objective criteria, such as productivity, may not be very reliable since they may be affected by external factors. The most serious objection, however, concerns validity. Many of the criteria are obviously inappropriate. For example, there is more to school and university than passing examinations, or so most people like to think; yet how can these other intangibles be measured? A truly satisfactory criterion cannot be discovered until there is complete agreement about what exactly the job or training is supposed to achieve; this in turn often requires extensive sociological analysis and generally some important value judgements about the structure of society. However, while no criterion is entirely satisfactory, it is often necessary to select the best available, for purposes of research or for refining selection procedures.

Once the criterion has been established, the selection procedure should be validated against it, that is, the selectors should see whether their judgements about the suitability of the candidates agree with the supervisors' ratings or the objective criterion. There are two ways of doing this. In the first, the selectors sort the candidates into those they would accept and those they would fail, possibly grading them as well. All candidates nevertheless are accepted, including those thought unsuitable. After a time their performance is assessed and the validity of the selectors' judgements determined. This method has the obvious snag that people thought unsuitable will be taken on, so it has not been used very often. More commonly the selectors grade the applicants and select the number they want from the top of the list. Subsequently, a correlation is calculated between the selector's grading and the criterion. This method is less satisfactory since nothing is known about the rejected candidates, some of whom may have proved successful. Furthermore, the correlation between selection, grade and criterion will tend to be small, since a limited range of candidates is included in the comparison. It is possible to 'correct' the correlation, that is, increase it, on the argument that a larger correlation would be obtained if a wider range of candidates were included in the comparison. There are other ways of assessing the predictive validity of a test, besides correlations (see Dunnette, 1966, for a review).

There is another reason why the correlations between selection and criterion tend to be low. It is a principle of validation studies that the validity correlation can never be larger than the reliability of the criterion. Thus if the validity of the eleven-plus examination is checked by correlating eleven-plus marks with GCE results, the correlation could not be larger than the correlation of the GCE itself, that is, its reliability. Put in simpler terms, if we have no really reliable way of measuring school achievement, we can scarcely hope to predict a pupil's achievement with perfect success. In fact, the criteria used to validate selection are likely to have only very modest reliabilities. Ratings of any sort are never very reliable, and objective indices, like productivity, are liable to be affected by a variety of factors, other than the employee's efficiency. It follows that validity coefficients will tend to be low.

Review of the work on selection

This section will concentrate on the interview as a selection method, with some mention of references and school assessments. Biographical data and academic achievement, as well as tests given by the selection staff, will be mentioned in comparison.

References and reports have some validity, although it is not always very high. For example, Furneau (1961) finds that headmasters' reports on university candidates correlated 0·30 with exam results, while the reports by candidate's sub-ject matter correlated 0·50. This is a reasonably large cor-relation, considering that the sample is highly selected. However, commanding officers' reports on candidates for Officer Cadets Training Unit correlated only 0·26 with the candidate's OCTU performance (Vernon and Parry, 1949).

There is very extensive literature on the interview, that has been reviewed by Mayfield (1964), Ulrich and Trumbo (1965) and Wagner (1949). The reliability of interview judge-ments is generally fair, ranging from 0·62 to 0·90, although Ulrich and Trumbo remark that 'with few exceptions [re-liabilities] are lower than usually accepted for devices used for individual prediction'. The evidence on validity is less encouraging. Ulrich and Trumbo find that validities of less than 0·50 are the rule and validities of less than 0·30 very common; even allowing for unreliable criteria and narrow spread of candidates, these correlations are very low. Some studies have found that the interview, combined with bio-graphical or test data, gives a better prediction than the data alone. For example, one study found that predictions of success at teaching, based on interview and other data, had some validity, whereas predictions based on the other data alone had no significant validity.

It is possible to calculate the 'wastage rate', that is, the number of good candidates rejected and the number of bad candidates accepted, given the validity coefficient and the selection ratio – the number of candidates to be accepted. The higher the validity of the selection procedure, the less wastage there will be. Table 3 shows the distribution of rejection and acceptance in relation to success or failure on the job, where the validity coefficient is 0·50 and half the candidates are accepted. The wastage rate is 34 per cent, of whom half are bad candidates who were accepted. Thus with this validity and selection ratio, one-third of the candidates selected will in fact be unsuccessful. If the selection ratio is lower, the picture changes. Table 4 shows the results obtained, with the validity still at 0·50, but with only one in five candidates being selected. The total wastage rate has gone down to 22 per cent, but the proportion of bad candidates accepted has increased, so that now more bad candidates are accepted than good. If the selection validity is lower than 0·50, the proportion of good to bad candidates decreases still further. Table 5 shows that a validity of 0·25 and a selection of one in five means that twice as many bad candidates will be accepted as good and also that twice as many good candidates will be rejected as accepted. In fact, selection is now scarcely better than chance; one would expect to get four good candidates out of twenty if one selected at random, whereas the selection method gives only six or seven.

Table 3
Percentage of Good and Bad Candidates Accepted and Rejected, where the Selection Procedure has a Validity of 0·50 and half the Candidates are Accepted

	good	bad
accepted	33	17
rejected	17	33

Table 4
Percentage of Good and Bad Candidates Accepted and Rejected, where the Selection Procedure has a Validity of 0·50 and One-Fifth of the Candidates are Accepted

	good	bad
accepted	9	11
rejected	11	69

Table 5

Percentage of Good and Bad Candidates Accepted and Rejected, where the Selection Procedure has a Validity of 0·25 and One-Fifth of the Candidates are Accepted

	good	bad
accepted	6	14
rejected	14	66

Improving the interview

It appears that in some circumstances – low validity and low selection ratio – the interview is rather a waste of time and that candidates might well be picked randomly. However, it is possible to improve the validity of the interview. Much of the fallibility of interviewing comes from interviewers who assume they are always right and who do not evaluate their procedures in any way. The literature on interviewing gives a number of pointers to ways of improving the validity.

1. Some interviewers are better than others. Handyside and Duncan (1954) find that different interviewers had individual validity coefficients ranging from 0·17 to 0·66. Vernon and Parry (1949) find that one Wren recruiting assistant had a validity of 0·55, whereas the objective test – generally superior to interviews – had a validity of only 0·39. It follows that the selectors should themselves be selected.

2. Interviewers can be trained and numerous training schemes are in operation, although not enough is known about their usefulness.

3. There is some evidence that two interviews may be better than one, although a third interview was not found to contribute anything.

4. Some large-scale procedures have used interviews in conjunction with other tests. In the WOSB, the candidate for officer training is interviewed several times by different people including a psychiatrist, and also participates in

ty. Nevertheless, it is possible to ask
e consistent and whether they are cor-

of the reliability of diagnosis have been
1964; Zubin, 1967). Most studies have
reliability, that is, whether two or more
out what is wrong with the patient or,
ther they agree about what treatment
in summarizes the evidence from six
ment on 'major' categories – organic,
haracter disorder – ranged from 64 per
greement on specific categories, that is,
or neurosis, was generally lower, ran-
t to 66 per cent. Zubin concludes that
degree of overall agreement between
th regard to specific diagnosis is too
gnosis. The overall agreement on gen-
gnosis, although somewhat higher, still
sired.' It is worth noting that the evi-
does not consider whether the patient
presumably if the diagnosis of which
is unreliable, the diagnosis of whether
e perfect. Studies of the reliability of
for service recruits, coastguards, etc.,
ecide whether the subject is ill at all,
liability. The reliability coefficients
6
iability can be attributed to the un-
categories and the difficulty of pro-
. Correct diagnosis of organic illness –
l deficiency, etc. – is generally higher,
conditions are more definite cat-
gnosis of neurosis is less reliable,
s of the category. Hunt, Wittson and
–retest reliability of 94 per cent when
whether naval recruits were fit for

various situational tests of leadership, etc. The validity of the combined tests is higher than the validity of any single one. A similar procedure has been used for selecting the administrative grades of the civil service (P. E. Vernon, 1950). The various interviews together have a validity of 0·49 compared with a validity of 0·45 for the situation tests, and 0·36 or 0·46 for observations of group discussions. The entire process has a validity of 0·50 to 0·62, for different groups. An individual test may have low validity but, if it does not cover the same ground as any other, may still be useful and contribute to the overall effectiveness of the selection.

5. It has been suggested that interviews are much better if the interviewer knows what he is looking for and reaches a number of specific decisions about specific points, rather than reaching a global decision about the candidate's suitability. Yonge (1956) rates the attitudes of a number of employees to their work using a rating schedule and finds that these correlated 0·70 with supervisors' ratings. Rimland (1960), in a study on the US Navy, finds that interviewers could assess the candidates' career motivation very well, but did not assess overall suitability very accurately. This is an example of how the interview, or any other method, can contribute one piece of information that is not enough by itself to reach a verdict, but which contributes to the overall picture. However, Mayfield (1964) points out that no study has been done that actually compared structured and unstructured interviews.

6. Validity can be improved still further if the interviewer not only looks for specific information, but looks for specific items whose relevance has been established by follow-up studies. Vernon and Parry (1949) describe lists of 'contra-indications' for candidates, established by follow-up methods. One list of contra-indications of responsibility included the following items:

Unsteady, unprogressive or retrogressive work record
Inability to give an intelligible account of own job

Post-war ambition below the level expected from pre-war job and test scores

Underachievement at school

No further education in connection with occupation, or otherwise, since leaving school

Dislike at school for maths and science and preference for handwork, athletics, geography, or no preference stated

Interests that are purely social, purely athletic, or entirely solitary, or are restless and migratory

Hypochondria

If a candidate shows more than a few of these signs he is unlikely to be suitable for any responsible service job.

Some of these contra-indications probably apply fairly generally, so it may not be necessary to do a special follow-up study for every selection procedure.

7. Investigations of the validity of survey interviews have shown that some information is more trustworthy than others. The respondent usually gives truthful or accurate details of his social and economic status, and invariably reports his sex correctly. Other information may not be reliable; in one study it was found that only half the candidates told the truth when asked if they had been to the 'Vocation Rehabilitation Agency', apparently thinking that this would prejudice the employer against them. The interviewer should not rely solely on what the interviewee tells him, therefore, but should have some biographical information as well. It has been found that intelligence or ability can be estimated reasonably accurately in the interview, unlike most other traits (Mayfield, 1964). It has also been established that interviewers are more influenced by unfavourable information and it has been suggested that the interview serves primarily as a search for disqualifying data about the candidate.

Most of the evidence described necessarily comes from studies conducted in large organizations, where many people are interviewed or selected for the same job. Similarly, many

of the meth
could only
pointed for
difficulty an
a large orga
obviously b
often be dor
the candidat
ably be high
person he w
may have so
will run his own p

Conclusion.
much on the w
by a competent
for and who uses
interview by an
forms a glo
his conclusi
well do no
dates at ra
tematic res
points out
turing of in
and the fo
investigate

Diagnosis

Selection
only a mi
the other
very impo
of diagn
made ab
sumed by
infallible

T–IP–G

reliability and valid
whether diagnoses a
rect.

Reliability

A number of studies
done (P. E. Vernon,
examined inter-rater
psychiatrists agree a
in some studies, wh
should be used. Zu
recent studies. Agre
functional, neurosis,
nt to 84 per cent.
rieties of psychosi
g from 38 per ce
indicates that th
ent observers
for individual di
eral categories of dia
leaves much to be d
dence Zubin discusse
is indeed mentally ill
illness the patient has
he is ill at all cannot
psychiatric 'screening
where the task is to
give rather better
range from 0.39 to 0.

Much of the unre
satisfactory diagnosti
ducing anything bette
senile dementia, ment
possibly because suc
egories, whereas di
reflecting the vaguene
Hunt (1953) find a tes
a psychiatrist decidec

service, compared with only 54 per cent agreement on major categories and 33 per cent on specific categories. Some dis-agreement, however, does result from differing perceptions of the patients. In one study thirty-five psychiatrists saw a film of a patient. Fourteen thought he was neurotic, while the other twenty-one thought he was psychotic; when the psychiatrists' reasons for diagnosis were analysed it turned out that those who thought the patient psychotic saw him as 'apathetic' while the others did not.

However, the psychiatrist's selection of appropriate treat-ment is also unreliable, ranging from 77 per cent agreement for organic complaints to 51 per cent for neurosis and 33 per cent for character disorders. Bannister, Salmon and Leiber-man (1964) find great disagreement when psychiatrists are asked to select the appropriate therapy for a given illness; the most popular choice for each case is chosen only 18 per cent of the time. The low reliability again probably reflects the unsatisfactory state of knowledge about mental illness as much as the psychiatrist's inaccuracy.

Validity

The study of the validity of diagnosis involves the criterion problem again. Mental illness is a vague concept, since the patient's health or illness is often defined by his ability to lead a normal life. Operational criteria can be used for the purpose of studying validity, but these are often un-satisfactory. Two criteria have been used, depending on the type of investigation. With psychiatric patients the criterion tends to be recovery, whereas in studies of psychiatric screening, for example, of service recuits, it tends to be breakdown. These are relatively crude, of course, but no other objective criterion is possible. It is not possible to per-form physical tests or any other sort of test on a patient and conclude that he is 'really' a paranoid schizophrenic; the only criterion for such a diagnosis is the psychiatrist's opinion. (Some studies have used as a criterion the opinion of another, more senior psychiatrist; this is obviously un-satisfactory.)

Studies of the first sort tend to take as their criterion discharge from hospital. This is not a very good criterion for three reasons. In the first place, the spontaneous remission rates for most forms of mental illness are very high, which will tend to obscure the issue. Secondly, discharge depends often on the psychiatrist's opinion about the patient, which is what is being evaluated. Thirdly, it has been found that only a third of discharged schizophrenics under sixty were working full time, which suggests that many had not adjusted satisfactorily, despite being discharged. However, Zubin cites some impressive evidence showing that psychiatrists could predict which schizophrenic patients would recover and that they gave these different diagnostic labels. Nearly all patients diagnosed as 'catatonic', 'mixed', 'undifferentiated', 'reactive', etc., recovered, while only a third of those diagnosed 'simple', 'paranoid', 'hebephrenic' and 'process' schizophrenics did. The original diagnostic categories devised by Kraepelin, were in fact intended to predict the outcome of the illness, as well as giving it a name. It appears, therefore, that psychiatrists cannot agree on the name to give a psychotic condition, but can tell whether the patient will recover.

Another (indirect) criterion of the validity of diagnosis is the effectiveness of treatment (although accurate diagnosis of, for example, cancer does not imply that treatment will succeed). It has been established that psychotherapy is not very effective, since just as many untreated control patients recover (two-thirds over three years) – a dispiriting conclusion that gives no evidence of the validity of diagnosis.

Studies of large-scale screening of service recruits, in Britain and the US, give rather more encouraging results (P. E. Vernon, 1964). For example, Hill and Williams (1947) find that a psychiatrist's diagnosis of neurotic predisposition is related to the recruit's subsequent career. Neurotic symptoms had been noted in 69 per cent of those who had psychiatric breakdowns and in 20 per cent of those who had accidents or became casualties but in only 5 per cent of those who completed their tour of duty successfully. Similar results have been reported for screening of paratroopers and

US Navy recruits. While the screening is not infallible, it is obviously well worthwhile, if 50 to 70 per cent of potential breakdowns can be detected before they happen. One study has been reported that suggests that screening could be done quite effectively by lay people. Wren recruiting assistants screened about three hundred subjects, half of whom were actually neurotic patients; they picked out 58 per cent of the neurotic and 16 per cent of the normals, as potential psychiatric cases. The neurotics they 'missed' mostly had affective symptoms; the hysterical patients were more easily identified. (The Wrens may have been so successful partly because they were given a list of contra-indications to look for.) However, a study of officers who had psychiatric breakdowns shows that the psychiatrists and psychologists at the selection board had tended to give adverse reports, suggesting that they had detected symptoms that the lay staff had missed.

Other forms of diagnosis or guidance

Psychiatrists are not the only people who form judgements about other people's problems and attempt to help them. Social workers and others try to help those with specific problems, while counselling and vocational guidance services offer advice to everyone about particular problems or choice of career. These judgements often involve important aspects of the subject's life and may have far-reaching consequences, so it is obviously essential that they should be as accurate and unbiased as possible.

Unfortunately, what little evidence there is suggests that such judgements are not always very satisfactory. P. E. Vernon (1964) describes several large-scale studies of the effectiveness of child guidance, none of which gives any evidence that child guidance makes a difference to the child's progress. Indeed, a suspiciously familiar two-thirds recovery rate in guided and unguided children was found in one study. One reason for the failure of effective child guidance may be the insistence on 'deep' quasi-psychoanalytic explantations; Phillips (1960) finds that a simple approach, giving the parents 'common-sense' explanations of problems and telling them what to do about them, produces better results than a longer course of 'depth' interviews. Sarbin (1943) finds that counsellors were not very good at predicting boys' school grades, but did better for girls; in both cases, however, predictions derived from school marks and IQ were as good or better. Weighted objective indices have been found better for predicting 'recidivism' – further criminal activity – in Borstal boys, than the Borstal governors' and masters' reports (Mannheim and Wilkins, 1955).

Vocational guidance, on the other hand, has proved quite useful. A follow-up study by the National Institute for Industrial Psychology (NIIP) looks at people who had taken jobs the NIIP advised them to take and compares them with people who had taken jobs which were not thought to be suitable; 92 per cent of the former were 'successful and happy' in their jobs as compared with only 57 per cent of the latter. Another study has shown that vocational guidance is only effective when carried out by experts; non-experts were quite unsuccessful at predicting what jobs would suit school-leavers.

Conclusion

The evidence on the usefulness of psychiatric and other professional diagnosis and guidance is not very reassuring. These important decisions are all too often completely unreliable and even the best results are far from perfect. Much of the inaccuracy can be attributed to the difficulty of the task or the unhelpful classification being used. Some, however, must be attributed to the failure of those making the judgements to try to evaluate their performance by follow-up studies, or to try to improve their judgements by using a wider range of information.

9 Summing Up

In this chapter we shall look back over the work we have described in the previous chapters and try to evaluate its success and its significance. We shall then try to draw some more general conclusions about the progress of research in the area and make some suggestions about how it should proceed in the future.

General review of work in interpersonal perception

Our first step in examining the question of interpersonal perception was to try to define its scope, to determine what sorts of judgements are made about other people. We concluded that a wide variety of judgements about others are made, although certain broad classifications can be given. For example, some judgements concern rapidly changing aspects of the individual, whereas others concern aspects that do not change. We also saw that some judgements are made deliberately and consciously, whereas others are made unconsciously.

The second step was to examine the various explanations put forward of the process of forming of judgements. Two types of explanation have been offered that were broadly described as 'intuition' and 'inference' explanations. The intuition approach proved to be obscure, unhelpful and in parts logically unsound. The inference approach, on the other hand, provides a useful conceptual framework for examining interpersonal perception (although it is not strictly a theory and does not generate any testable predictions).

The inference model suggests that judgements can be considered as syllogisms and that they, therefore, depend on general principles about personality and behaviour, that the judge considers to hold good. These general principles or 'inference rules' form the first step in making the judgement. They have also been studied extensively and profitably by a variety of methods. The research on inference rules was described in chapters 3 and 4.

One aspect of inference rule systems that we noticed in chapters 3 and 4 is their frequent inaccuracy. Many inference rules are incorrect or biased and hence likely to lead to incorrect judgements. The next two chapters were concerned with the question of accuracy. Accuracy of perception has been studied as extensively as rule systems, but less profitably. In chapter 5 we discussed the various methods that have been used and observed that they are subject to many disadvantages. Because of the disadvantages relatively little has emerged, although some findings are listed in chapter 6.

The remaining two chapters were also largely concerned with accuracy of perception. Chapter 7 was concerned with the generality of the ability to judge accurately across a variety of situations and with the characteristics of people who are able to judge others accurately. Some interesting suggestions emerge from this research, but insufficient work has been done since to confirm them.

Chapter 8 looked at practical applications of interpersonal perception in interviewing, psychiatric diagnosis and related areas, again principally considering the accuracy of perception. Some rather alarming results emerged, showing that important judgements made frequently about people in work and other situations are very often quite inaccurate. Some of the reasons for this inaccuracy were discussed and it was seen that many people take accuracy of judgement for granted and rarely try to assess their own performance.

More general conclusions emerging from research

From the review above, one general conclusion emerges fairly clearly, namely that research in some areas has been more profitable than in others. Research on inference rules has reached a number of interesting conclusions. For example, we have seen that apparently independent characteristics tend to be associated in the minds of many observers, often to a surprising extent. It has been suggested that three independent factors can account for most of our thinking about others – even though there are eighteen thousand different trait names in the English language. Even if we do not accept that there are three factors, there is no doubt that thinking about others is much less complex than we generally suppose. We also saw that many of the associations between characteristics, implied by the use of broad dimensions, are in fact unjustified.

Similarly, the research on 'identification rules' has been very fruitful. A considerable amount is now known about the use made, and the usefulness of, a variety of cues: facial expression, tone of voice, posture, gesture and orientation, direction of gaze, etc. We may note, however, that research on identification rules is not as far advanced as that on 'association rules'; it has started more recently and also has far more ground to cover. It takes longer to study identification rules since the methods required are more laborious; association rules, on the other hand, can be studied using paper and pencil methods.

When we come to consider the progress of research on accuracy of perception, we find a quite different state of affairs. A large amount of research has been reported, but it has not reached very many sound conclusions. This is largely because of defects in the methods used, that have made the results of experiments hard to interpret. The defects are mostly associated with choice of criterion and with the judgement task and scoring systems used. A number of studies may not have been measuring accuracy of judgement of different people at all, but the ability to identify the commonest response to a particular task. However, we have argued in chapter 5 that the problems are not insuperable, and ought not to prevent further research being undertaken.

We have noted that research on inference rules has been very successful, whereas research on accuracy has been relatively unsuccessful. These are the two most important aspects of interpersonal perception – *how* we form judgements and *how good* we are at forming judgements. However, there are several other areas where research, successful or otherwise, has not flourished at all. The most notable example of neglect is the content of judgements; the question of what judgements we make has been largely ignored. Experimenters have given their subjects judgement tasks without considering whether the particular type of judgement involved is made frequently or at all. We shall give a list of other neglected topics – large and small – in the third section.

We may draw a second and related general conclusion. Interpersonal perception, like other areas of social psychology, has suffered from a 'triumph of method over subject matter', to paraphrase a well-known remark. A large number of studies in the literature seem to have been done because the method was convenient, or easy, or popular, not because they were worth doing. Once a method had been devised and had caught on, large numbers of experiments were done using the same method and employing often very trivial variations on the same theme. Thus there are a very large number of studies in the literature on the recognition of emotion expressed facially. Most of these studies have used still photographs, which we have seen are not a very good means of presentation. Only a few studies have used films, which are greatly superior and have been available for most of the time under consideration. Other methods that have been very popular include the empathy method and the trait-rating method.

Consideration of the popularity of empathy and trait-rating methods draws us to another conclusion, about the role of method in social psychology. These two methods enjoyed considerable popularity in the twenty years before 1955, despite their obvious drawbacks. When the attention was called to these snags, by Cronbach and others, they ceased to be used. As a result few studies of accuracy of perception, or related issues, have been reported in the last ten or twelve years. Because existing methods proved unsatisfactory, the topic was abandoned. No attempt has been made to improve the methods to eliminate the defects or to devise new methods although, as we have tried to show in chapter 5, this would not be difficult.

Since the mid-fifties, interest on interpersonal perception has been focused on the inference process and on inference rules. A cynical observer might suggest that inference rules have been studied extensively because accuracy proved hard to study and because convenient methods for studying inference rules were devised. (It is instructive to remember the date of origin of the methods most commonly used in current interpersonal perception work. The Role Repertory Grid dates from 1955, the semantic differential from 1957 and the cue trait method from 1956. Only the 'impression formation' method – presentation of lists of adjectives – goes back earlier, to 1946.) The research on inference rules has been very valuable, of course, but we are left with the impression that it has been done because convenient methods are readily to hand, not because it was considered important *a priori*.

The emphasis on convenience of method has tended to result in experiments that have little external validity or whose external validity is unproved. Perhaps the best example of this is the impression formation literature. In these studies, different lists of adjectives are presented to the subject and the variations in the composition and order of the list are reflected in ratings. Such studies are justified on the grounds that they provide a rigorous investigation of the processes of integration of information in interpersonal perception. However, we may object that we do not usually receive information about others in the form of lists of adjectives – especially not the vague adjectives commonly used in these studies – nor do we give our opinion in the form of ratings. Of course, we sometimes get information in written form, in letters, references, testimonials, reports, etc., so impression formation studies have some direct relevance; they can, furthermore, be taken to give us information about the integration of other sorts of information and thus tell us how all information integration in interpersonal perception occurs. This argument is implausible, however, since the literature has shown that minute variations in the composition or order of the list or in the timing of the judgement task completely change the final impression. For example, embedding the adjectives in two different simple sentence structures or requiring the judge to give an opinion after each adjective or after he has heard them all can alter the final impression considerably. If minor variations in the experimental task can affect the results, it seems unlikely that the method can have much external validity.

To conclude this section, it can be argued that interpersonal perception, as a field of research, is too method-dependent and that this has two undesirable consequences. In the first place, issues are studied because they are easy to study, rather than because they are important. If an important issue is hard to study, it will be neglected. Secondly, some of the methods in general use are somewhat narrow and appear to be lacking in external validity.

Directions for future research

To some extent our recommendations for future progress in this area follow on from what has been said in the previous section. They fall into two sections – method and subject matter. We have seen that research currently concentrates on inference rules – and more particularly on the number of independent factors that may be extracted from them – and that it formerly concentrated on accuracy. We have also observed that these are the two most important issues in the field. The third most important issue – what judgements we actually make and what form they take – has not received its fair share of attention in research, even though it could be plausibly argued that this question should be answered first. Perhaps we have been premature in devising a model to explain judgements before we know what needs explaining. Perhaps we have been even more premature in studying the accuracy with which particular judgements are made, if in fact people never make judgements of that sort. Let us suppose, for example, that people do not ordinarily make judgements in terms of general personality traits, but only try to predict specific behaviour. It follows that a great deal of time and effort has been wasted on trait-rating studies and that attempts to devise better ways of doing trait-rating studies would also be a waste of time.

The actual content and form of judgements made about other people is perhaps the most seriously neglected area. We can point to a number of other interesting questions that have not received as much attention as they merit. Some are major omissions – like the content of judgements – and would require new methods to be devised to study them, whereas others are less extensive and could be studied by existing methods.

Perhaps the most obvious line of research to pursue concerns the 'good judge of others'. As we saw in chapter 7, research on generality of ability and on the characteristics of good judges of others ceased when interest in accuracy waned, even though very interesting results were reported by Bronfenbrenner, Harding and Gallway (1958) and others. It is particularly unfortunate that the question of generality of ability has been left unsettled since Cline and Richards and Crow and Hammond produced their conflicting results. Various other questions about accuracy of judgement could also profitably be studied – the perception of intelligence for example. Much more research also needs to be done using Cline's Behaviour Postdiction Test and similar methods. Further research on the perception of transient states in social interaction needs to be done. This research should use less artificial methods than those used in most studies so far and should study a wider range of judgements.

The research on accuracy and the 'good judge' would largely be a continuation of existing research, using existing methods or improved versions of them. In chapter 2 we suggested that some attempt should be made to bring person perception closer to visual perception in general, using methods taken from visual perception studies. We suggested that measures of the time taken to form various sorts of judgements would throw some further light on the processes involved. We also suggested that some investigation should be made into the suggestion that there are two parallel channels in operation in interpersonal perception. Research on these two questions could prove to be very valuable, but would require entirely new methods, that would need extensive development first.

In chapter 3 we discussed various aspects of inference rules and saw that some of these aspects, like 'cognitive complexity', had been studied very extensively. Other aspects of inference rules have not been studied in such detail. For example, we had little to report about the origin of inference rules, except some interesting but speculative observations by Sarbin, Taft and Bailey (1960) and a few incidental findings. The study of the origins of inference rules would be very enlightening in itself and would contribute to other problems that have also not been studied to any great extent. How are socially undesirable inference rules like racial stereotypes acquired? How easy is it to change someone's inference rules? Indeed the question of origin is closely related to the questions of rigidity and change.

Conclusions

We have seen that the study of certain areas of interpersonal perception has been very profitable, whereas the study of other areas has not been so successful. We have also commented that some areas have been relatively neglected. One possible reason for this neglect is the predominant influence of method in the study of interpersonal perception. We have suggested that this is a bad thing, especially since some of the methods involved are of dubious validity. The study of interpersonal perception can best be advanced by putting the problem before the method.

References

ALLPORT, G. W. (1961), *Pattern and Growth in Personality*, Harper & Row.

ALLPORT, G. W., and ODBERT, H. S. (1936), 'Trait names: a psycho-lexical study', *Psychol. Monogr.*, vol. 47, no. 211.

ANDERSON, N. H. (1965), 'Primacy effects in personality impression formation using a specialised order effect paradigm', *J. Person. soc. Psychol.*, vol. 2, pp. 1–9.

ARGYLE, M. (1969), *Social Interaction*, Methuen.

ARGYLE, M., and DEAN, J. (1965), 'Eye contact, distance and affiliation', *Sociometry*, vol. 28, pp. 289–304.

ARGYLE, M., and KENDON, A. (1967), 'The experimental analysis of social performance', *Adv. exp. soc. Psychol.*, vol. 3, pp. 55–98.

ARGYLE, M., and McHENRY, R. (1971), 'Do spectacles really affect our judgements of intelligence?', *Brit. J. soc. clin. Psychol.*, vol. 10, pp. 27–9.

ARGYLE, M., and WILLIAMS, M. (1969), 'Observer-observed, a reversible perspective in person perception', *Sociometry*, vol. 32, pp. 396–412.

ARGYLE, M., SALTER, V., BURGESS, P., NICHOLSON, N. C., and WILLIAMS, M. (1970), 'The communication of inferior and superior attitudes by verbal and non-verbal signals', *Bull. de Psychol.*, vol. 23, pp. 540–48.

ARNHEIM, R. (1949), 'The Gestalt theory of expression', *Psychol. Rev.*, vol. 56, pp. 156–71.

ASCH, S. E. (1946), 'Forming impressions of personality', *J. abnorm. soc. Psychol.*, vol. 41, pp. 258–90.

AUSTIN, J. L. (1962), *Sense and Sensibilia*, Oxford University Press.

BANNISTER, D. (1962), 'The nature and measurement of schizophrenic thought disorder', *J. ment. Sci.*, vol. 108, pp. 825–30.

BANNISTER, D., SALMON, P., and LEIBERMAN, D. M. (1964), 'Diagnosis–treatment relationships in psychiatry: a statistical analysis', *Brit. J. Psychiat.*, vol. 110, pp. 726–32.

BIERI, J. (1953), 'Changes in interpersonal perceptions following social interaction', *J. abnorm. soc. Psychol.*, vol. 48, pp. 61–6.

BIERI, J. (1955), 'Cognitive complexity–simplicity and predictive behavior', *J. abnorm. soc. Psychol.*, vol. 51, pp. 263–8.

BIRDWHISTELL, R. F. (1968), 'Kinesics', *International Encyclopedia of the Social Sciences*, vol. 8, pp. 379–85.

BONARIUS, C. J. (1965), 'Research on the personal construct theory of George A. Kelly: construct repertory test and basic theory', *Prog. exp. Person. Res.*, vol. 2, pp. 2–46.

BRONFENBRENNER, U., HARDING, J., and GALLWAY, M. (1958), 'The measurement of skill in social perception', in D. C. McClelland (ed.), *Talent and Society*, Van Nostrand.

BROWN, R. (1965), *Social Psychology*, Free Press.

BRUNER, J. S., SHAPIRO, D., and TAGIURI, R. (1958), 'The meaning of traits in isolation and in combination', in R. Tagiuri and L. Petrullo (eds.), *Person Perception and Interpersonal Behavior*, Stanford University Press.

BRUNSWIK, E., and REITER, L. (1937), 'Eindrucks-Charaktere schematisierter Gesichter', *Z. Psych.*, vol. 142, pp. 67–134.

CHAMBERS, G. S., and HAMLIN, R. M. (1957), 'The validity of judgements based on "blind" Rorschach records', *J. consult. Psychol.*, vol. 21, pp. 105–9.

CHANCE, J. E., and MEADERS, W. (1960), 'Needs and interpersonal perception', *J. Person.*, vol. 28, pp. 200–211.

CHELSEA, L. (1965), 'A study of implicit personality theories', unpublished paper cited by H. C. Smith, *Sensitivity to People*, McGraw-Hill, 1966.

CLINE, V. B. (1964), 'Interpersonal perception', *Prog. exp. Person. Res.*, vol. 1, pp. 221–84.

CLINE, V. B., and RICHARDS, J. M. (1960), 'Accuracy of interpersonal perception – a general trait', *J. abnorm. soc. Psychol.*, vol. 50, pp. 183–92.

CONDON, W. S., and OGSTON, W. D. (1966), 'Sound film analysis of normal and pathological behavior patterns', *J. nerv. ment. Dis.*, vol. 143, pp. 338–47.

COOK, M. (1969), 'Anxiety, speech disturbance and speech rate', *Brit. J. soc. clin. Psychol.*, vol. 8, pp. 13–21.

COOK, M. (1970), 'Experiments on orientation and proxemics', *Hum. Rel.*, vol. 23, pp. 261–76.

CROCKETT, W. H. (1965), 'Cognitive complexity and impression formation', *Prog. exp. Person. Res.*, vol. 2, pp. 47–90.

CRONBACH, L. J. (1955), 'Process affecting scores on "understanding others" and "assumed similarity" ', *Psychol. Bull.*, vol. 52, pp. 177–93.

CROW, W. J. (1957), 'The effects of training upon variability and accuracy in interpersonal perception', *J. abnorm. soc. Psychol.*, vol. 55, pp. 355–9.

CROW, W. J., and HAMMOND, K. R. (1957), 'The generality of accuracy and response sets in interpersonal perception', *J. abnorm. soc. Pyschol.*, vol. 54, pp. 384–90.

DARWIN, C. (1872), *The Expression of the Emotions in Man and Animals*, Murray.

DAVITZ, J. R. (1964), *The Communication of Emotional Meaning*, McGraw-Hill.

DITTMAN, A. T., and WYNNE, L. C. (1961), 'Linguistic analysis and the communication of emotionality in interviews', *J. abnorm. soc. Psychol.*, vol. 63, pp. 201–4.

DUNNETTE, M. D. (1966), *Personnel Selection and Placement*, Tavistock.

DYMOND, R. F. (1950), 'Personality and empathy', *J. consult. Psychol.*, vol. 14, pp. 343–50.

DYMOND, R. F., HUGHES, A. S., and RAABE, V. L. (1952), 'Measurable changes in empathy with age', *J. consult. Psychol.*, vol. 16, pp. 202–6.

EKMAN, P. (1965), 'Communication through non-verbal behavior: a source of information about an interpersonal relationship', in S. S. Tomkins and C. Izzard (eds.), *Affect, Cognition and Personality*, Springer Publishing Co.

EKMAN, P. (1969), 'Studies in non-verbal behaviour', paper read at NATO Symposium on Non-Verbal Communication, Oxford.

EKMAN, P., and FRIESEN, W. V. (1969), 'Origin, usage and coding: the basis of five categories in non-verbal behaviour', *Semiotica*, vol. 1, pp. 49–98.

EKMAN, P., SORENSON, F. R., and FRIESEN, W. V. (1969), 'Pan-cultural elements in facial displays of emotion', *Science*, vol. 164, pp. 86–8.

EXLINE, R. V. (1966), 'The effects of cognitive difficulty and cognitive style upon eye to eye contact in interactions', unpublished paper, University of Delaware.

EXLINE, R. V., and WINTERS, L. C., (1965), 'Affective relations and mutual glances in dyads' in S. S. Tomkins and C. Izzard (eds.), *Affect, Cognition and Personality*, Springer Publishing Co.

FIEDLER, F. E. (1964), 'A contingency model of leadership effectiveness', *Adv. exp. soc. Psychol.*, vol. 1, pp. 150–91.

FRENKEL–BRUNSWIK, E. (1939), 'Mechanisms of self-deception', *J. soc. Psychol.*, vol. 10, pp. 408–20.

FRIEDMAN, N. (1967), *The Social Nature of Psychological Research*, Basic Books.

FRIJDA, N. A. (1958), 'Facial expression and situational cues', *J. abnorm. soc. Psychol.*, vol. 57, pp. 149–55.

FRIJDA, N. A. (1969), 'Recognition of emotion', *Adv. exp. soc. Psychol.* vol. 4, pp. 167–225.

FURNEAU, W. D. (1961), *The Chosen Few*, Oxford University Press.

GAGE, N. L. (1952), 'Judging interests from expressive behavior', *Psychol. Monogr.*, vol. 66, no. 350.

GIBBINS, K. (1969), 'Communication aspects of women's clothes and their relation to fashionability', *Brit. J. soc. clin. Psychol.*, vol. 8, pp. 301–12.

GIBSON, J. J. (1950), *The Perception of the Visual World*, Houghton Mifflin.

GIEDT, F. H. (1955), 'Comparison of visual, content and auditory cues in interviewing', *J. consult. Psychol.*, vol. 19, pp. 407–16.

GOFFMAN, E. (1956), *The Presentation of Self in Everyday Life*, Edinburgh University Press.

GOLDMAN-EISLER, F. (1968), *Psycholinguistics: Experiments in Spontaneous Speech*, Academic Press.

GOLLIN, E. S. (1954), 'Forming impressions of personality', *J. Person.*, vol. 23, pp. 65–76.

GOUGH, H. G. (1948), 'A sociological theory of psychopathy', *Amer. J. Sociol.*, vol. 53, pp. 359–66.

GOUGH, H. G. and PETERSEN, D. R. (1952), 'The identification and measurement of predispositional factors in crime and delinquency', *J. consult. Psychol.*, vol. 16, pp. 207–12.

GREGORY, R. L. (1966), *Eye and Brain: The Psychology of Seeing*, World University Library.

GROSSMAN, B. A (1963), 'The measurement and determinants of interpersonal sensitivity', unpublished M.A. thesis, Michigan State University.

GUILFORD, J. P. (1929), 'An experiment in learning to read facial expressions', *J. abnorm. soc. Psychol.*, vol. 24, pp. 191–202.

HAGGARD, F. A., and ISAACS, K. S. (1966), 'Micromomentary facial expressions as indicators of ego-mechanisms in psychotherapy', in L. A. Gottschalk and A. H. Auerbach (eds.) *Methods of Research in Psychotherapy*, Appleton-Century-Crofts.

HALL, E. T. (1964), 'Silent assumptions in social communication', *Res. Pub. Assn Nerv. Ment. Dis.*, vol. 42, pp. 41–55.

HANDYSIDE, J. D., and DUNCAN, D. C. (1954), 'Four years later: a follow-up on an experiment in selecting superiors', *Occup. Psychol.*, vol. 28, pp. 9–23.

HATCH, R. S. (1962), *An Evaluation of a Forced Choice Differential Accuracy Approach to the Measurements of Supervisors' Empathy*, Prentice-Hall.

HEBB, D. O. (1946), 'Emotion in man and animals: an analysis of the intuitive processes of recognition', *Psychol. Rev.*, vol. 53, pp. 88–106.

HEIDER, F. (1958), *The Psychology of Interpersonal Behavior*, Wiley.

HEIDER, F., and SIMMEL, M. (1944), 'An experimental study of apparent behavior', *Amer. J. Psychol.*, vol. 57, pp. 243–59.

HOLMES, D. S., and BERKOWITZ, L. (1961), 'Some context effects in social perception', *J. abnorm. soc. Psychol.*, vol. 62, pp. 150–52.

HORNSTEIN, M. G. (1967), 'Accuracy of emotional communication and interpersonal compatibility', *J. Person.*, vol. 35, pp. 20–30.

HUNT, W. A., WITTSON, C. L., and HUNT, E. B. (1953),
'A theoretical and practical analysis of the diagnostic process',
in P. H. Hoch and J. Zubin (eds.), *Current Problems in Psychiatric
Diagnosis*, Grune & Stratton.

JECKER, J. D., MACCOBY, N., and BREITROSE, H. S. (1965),
'Improving accuracy in interpreting non-verbal cues of
comprehension', *Psychol. Schools*, vol. 2, pp. 239–44.

KAHN, R. L., and CANNELL, C. F. (1957), *The Dynamics of
Interviewing*, Wiley.

KELLEY, H. H. (1950), 'The warm–cold variable in first impressions of
persons', *J. Person.*, vol. 18, pp. 431–9.

KELLY, G. A. (1955), *The Psychology of Personal Constructs*,
Norton.

KENDON, A. (1967), 'Some functions of gaze-direction in social
interaction', *Acta. Psychol.*, vol. 26, pp. 1–47.

KENDON, A. (1968), 'Some observations on interactional synchrony',
unpublished paper, Project on Human Communication, Bronx
State Hospital.

KENDON, A., and COOK, M. (1969), 'The consistency of gaze patterns
in social interaction', *Brit. J. Psychol.*, vol. 60, pp. 481–94.

KRAMER, E. (1963), 'Judgements of personal characteristics and
emotions from non-verbal properties of speech', *Psychol. Bull.*,
vol. 60, pp. 408–20.

KRASNER, L. (1958), 'Studies of the verbal conditioning of behavior',
Psychol. Bull., vol. 55, pp. 148–70.

KRECH, D., CRUTCHFIELD, R. S., and BALLACHEY, E. L. (1962),
Individual in Society, McGraw-Hill.

KROUT, M. H. (1954), 'An experimental attempt to determine the
significance of unconscious manual symbolic movements',
J. gen. Psych., vol. 51, pp. 121–52.

KUTNER, B., WILLIAMS, C., and YARROW, P. R. (1952), 'Verbal
attitudes and overt behavior involving racial prejudice',
J. abnorm. soc. Psychol., vol. 47, pp. 647–52.

LALLJEE, M. G. (1967), 'On the classification of voices', unpublished
paper, University of Oxford.

LALLJEE, M. G., and COOK, M. (1969), 'An experimental
investigation of the function of filled pauses in speech',
Lang. Speech, vol. 12, pp. 24–8.

LALLJEE, M. G., and WILLIAMS, M. (1967), 'Speech rate and speech
disturbance in the perception of anxiety', unpublished paper,
University of Oxford.

LANDIS, L. (1929), 'Studies of emotional reactions: III. General
behavior and facial expressions', *J. comp. Psychol.*, vol. 4,
pp. 447–509.

LANGFELD, J. S. (1918), 'Judgements of facial expression and
suggestion', *Psychol. Rev.*, vol. 25, pp. 488–94.

LAY, C. H., and JACKSON, D. N. (1969), 'Analysis of the generality of trait-inferential relationships', *J. Person. soc. Psychol.*, vol. 12, pp. 12–21.

LAZARUS, R. S. (1969), 'Stress and emotion', paper read at XIII International Congress of Psychology, London.

LEVY, P. K. (1964), 'The ability to express and perceive vocal communications of feeling', in J. R. Davitz (ed.), *The Communication of Emotional Meaning*, McGraw-Hill.

LIBERMAN, P. (1965), 'On the acoustic basis of the perception of intonation by linguists', *Word*, vol. 21, pp. 40–54.

LITTLE, B.R. (1968a), 'Factors affecting the use of psychological vs. non-psychological constructs on the Rep Test', *Bull. Brit. Psychol. Soc.*, vol. 21, p. 34.

LITTLE, B. R. (1968b), 'Psychospecialisation: functions of differential interests in persons and things', *Bull. Brit. Psychol. Soc.*, vol. 21, p. 113.

LITTLE, B. R. (1968c), 'Sex differences and comparability of three measures of cognitive complexity', *Psychol. Rep.*, vol. 24, pp. 607–9.

LUCHINS, A. S. (1959), 'Primacy–recency in impression formation', in *The Order of Presentation in Persuasion*, Yale University Press.

LUNDY, R. M. (1956), 'Assimilative projection and accuracy of prediction in interpersonal perception', *J. abnorm. soc. Psychol.*, vol. 52, pp. 33–8.

McKEACHIE, W. J. (1952), 'Lipstick as a determiner of first impressions of personality', *J. soc. Psychol.*, vol. 36, pp. 241–4.

MACLAY, H., and OSGOOD, C. E. (1959), 'Hesitation phenomena in spontaneous English speech', *Word*, vol. 15, pp. 19–44.

MAIER, N. R. F. (1966), 'Sensitivity to attempts at deception in an interview situation', *Personn. Psychol.*, vol. 19, pp. 55–66.

MAIER, N. R. F., and JANTZEN, J. C. (1967), 'Reliability of reasons used in making judgements of honesty and dishonesty', *Percept. mot. Skills*, vol. 25, pp. 141–57.

MAIER, N. R. F., and THURBER, J. A. (1968), 'Accuracy of judgements of deception when an interview is watched, heard and read', *Personn. Psychol.*, vol. 21, pp. 23–30.

MANNHEIM, H., and WILKINS, C. T. (1955), *Prediction Methods in Relation to Borstal Training*, HMSO.

MASELLI, M. D., and ALTROCCHI, T. (1969), 'Attribution of intent', *Psychol. Bull.*, vol. 71, pp. 445–54.

MATARAZZO, J. D., and SASLOW, G. (1961), 'Differences in interview interaction behavior among normal and deviant groups', in C. A. Berg and C. M. Bass (eds.) *Conformity and Deviation*, Harper & Row.

MAYFIELD, E. C. (1964), 'The selection interview: a re-evaluation of published research', *Personn. Psychol.*, vol. 17, pp. 239–60.

MEHRABIAN, A. (1969), 'Significance of posture and position in the communication of attitude and status relationships', *Psychol. Bull.*, vol. 71, pp. 359–72.

MILGRAM, N. A. (1960), 'Cognitive and empathetic factors in role taking by schizophrenic and brain-damaged patients', *J. abnorm. soc. Psychol.*, vol. 60, pp. 219–24.

MINTZ, N. L. (1956), 'Effects of esthetic surroundings: II. Prolonged and repeated experience in a "beautiful" and "ugly" room', *J. Psychol.*, vol. 41, pp. 459–66.

MISCHEL, W. (1968), *Personality and Assessment*, Wiley.

MUNN, N. L. (1940), 'The effect of knowledge of situation upon judgement of emotion from facial expressions', *J. abnorm. soc. Psychol.*, vol. 35, pp. 324–38.

MURSTEIN, B. I., and PRYER, R. S. (1959), 'The concept of projection: a review', *Psychol. Bull.*, vol. 56, pp. 353–74.

NORSWORTHY, N. (1910), 'The validity of judgements of character', in J. Dewey (ed.), *Essays Philosophical and Psychological in Honour of William James*, Longman.

OSGOOD, C. E., SUCI, C. J., and TANNENBAUM, R. H. (1957), *The Measurement of Meaning*, Illinois University Press.

OSTWALD, P. F. (1965), 'Acoustic methods in psychiatry', *Sci. Amer.*, vol. 212, pp. 82–91.

PHILLIPS, E. L. (1960), 'Parent–child psychotherapy: a follow-up study using two techniques', *J. Psychol.*, vol. 49, pp. 195–202.

PIAGET, J. (1932), *The Moral Judgment of the Child*, Routledge & Kegan Paul, Free Press edn, 1956.

PITTENGER, R. E., HOCKETT, C. F., and DANEHY, J. J. (1960), *The First Five Minutes*, Martineau.

POLLACK, I., RUBINSTEIN, R., and HOROWITZ, A. (1960), 'Communication of verbal modes of expression', *Lang. Speech*, vol. 3, pp. 121–30.

PORTER, E. R., ARGYLE, M., and SALTER, V. (1970), 'What is signalled by proximity', *Percept. mot. Skills*, vol. 30, pp. 39–42.

REID, T. (1764), 'Inquiry into the human mind and the principles of common sense', in *The Works of Thomas Reid*, Mclachlan & Stewart.

RIMLAND, B. (1960), 'A follow-up analysis of the composite system for selecting NROTC students', *US Navy Bureau of Naval Personnel, Technical Bulletin*, no. 60-8.

ROKEACH, M. (1945), 'Studies in beauty: II. Some determinants of the perception of beauty in women', *J. soc. Psychol.*, vol. 22, pp. 155–69.

RYLE, G. (1949), *The Concept of the Mind*, Hutchinson.

SACKETT, G. R. (1965), 'Monkeys reared in isolation with pictures as visual input: evidence for an innate releasing mechanism', *Science*, vol. 154, pp. 1468–73.

SAINSBURY, P. (1955), 'Gestural movement during the psychiatric interview', *Psychosom. Med.*, vol. 17, pp. 458–69.

SARBIN, T. R. (1943), 'A contribution to the study of actuarial and individual methods of prediction', *Amer. J. Sociol.*, vol. 48, pp. 593–602.

SARBIN, T. R., TAFT, R., and BAILEY, D. E. (1960), *Clinical Inference and Cognitive Theory*, Holt, Rinehart & Winston.

SCHEFLEN, A. E. (1964), 'The significance of posture in communication systems', *Psychiatry*, vol. 27, pp. 316–31.

SCHLOSBERG, H. (1954), 'Three dimensions of emotion', *Psychol. Rev.*, vol. 61, pp. 81–8.

SCODEL, A., and MUSSEN, P. (1953), 'Social perception of authoritarians and non-authoritarians', *J. abnorm. soc. Psychol.*, vol. 48, pp. 181–4.

SEARS, R. R. (1936), 'Experimental studies of projection: attribution of traits', *J. soc. Psychol.*, vol. 7, pp. 151–63.

SECHREST, L., and JACKSON, D. N. (1961), 'Social intelligence and accuracy of interpersonal predictions', *J. Person.*, vol. 29, pp. 167–82.

SECORD, P. F. (1958), 'The role of facial features in interpersonal perception', in R. Tagiuri and L. Petrullo (eds.), *Person Perception and Interpersonal Behavior*, Stanford University Press.

SECORD, P. F., and BACKMAN, C. W. (1961), 'Personality theory and the problem of stability and change in individual behavior', *Psychol. Rev.*, vol. 68, pp. 21–32.

SECORD, P. F., and BACKMAN, C. W. (1964), *Social Psychology*, McGraw-Hill.

SOMMER, R. (1967), 'Small group ecology', *Psychol. Bull.*, vol. 67, pp. 145–52.

SPRANGER, E. (1928), *Types of Men*, Niemeyer.

STANTON, F., and BAKER, K. H. (1942), 'Interviewer bias and the recall of incompletely learned material', *Sociometry*, vol. 5, pp. 123–34.

STEINER, R. T. (1955), 'Interpersonal behavior as influenced by accuracy of social perception', *Psychol. Rev.*, vol. 62, pp. 268–74.

✓ STOTLAND, E. (1969), 'Exploratory investigations of empathy', *Adv. exp. soc. Psychol.* vol. 4, pp. 271–314.

STRONGMAN, K. T., and HART, C. J. (1968), 'Stereotyped reactions to body build', *Psychol. Rep.*, vol. 23, pp. 1175–8.

TAFT, R. (1955), 'The ability to judge people,' *Psychol. Bull.*, vol. 52, pp. 1–23.

TAFT, R. (1956), 'Some characteristics of good judges of others', *Brit. J. Psychol.*, vol. 47, pp. 19–29.

TAFT, R. (1966), 'Accuracy of empathic judgements of acquaintances and strangers', *J. Person. soc. Psychol.*, vol. 3, pp. 600–604.

TAGIURI, R. (1958), 'Social preference and its perception', in R. Tagiuri and L. Petrullo (eds.), *Person Perception and Interpersonal Behavior*, Stanford University Press.

TAGIURI, R. (1969), 'Person perception', in G. Lindzey and, E. Aronson (eds.), *The Handbook of Social Psychology*, vol. 3 Addison-Wesley.

TAGIURI, R., and KOGAN, N. (1957), 'The visibility of interpersonal preferences', *Hum. Relat.*, vol. 10, pp. 385–90.

THIBAUT, J. W., and RIECKEN, A. W. (1955), 'Some determinants and consequences of the perception of social causality', *J. Person.*, vol. 24, pp. 113–33.

THOMPSON, D. F., and MELTZER, L. (1964), 'Communication of emotional intent by facial expression', *J. abnorm. soc. Psychol.*, vol. 68, pp. 129–35.

THORNTON, G. R. (1944), 'The effect of wearing glasses on judgements of personality traits of people seen briefly', *J. appl. Psychol.*, vol. 28, pp. 203–7.

TOCH, H. H., RABIN, A. I., and WILKINS, D. M. (1962), 'Factors entering into ethnic identifications: an experimental study', *Sociometry*, vol. 25, pp. 297–312.

TRAVERS, R. M. W. (1943), 'The general ability to judge group knowledge', *Amer. J. Psychol.*, vol. 56, pp. 95–9.

ULRICH, L., and TRUMBO, D. (1965), 'The selection interview since 1949', *Psychol. Bull.*, vol. 63, pp. 100–116.

VERNON, M. D. (1952), *A Further Study of Visual Perception*, Cambridge University Press.

VERNON, P. E. (1933), 'Some characteristics of the good judge of personality', *J. soc. Psychol.*, vol. 4, pp. 42–58.

VERNON, P. E. (1950), 'The validation of Civil Service Selection Board procedures', *Occup. Psychol.*, vol. 25, pp. 75–95.

VERNON, P. E. (1964), *Personality Assessment*, Methuen.

VERNON, P. E., and PARRY, J. B. (1949), *Personnel Selection in the British Forces*, University of London Press.

VINE, I. (1969), 'Communication by facial-visual signals', in J. H. Crook (ed.), *Social Behavior in Animals and Men*, Academic Press.

WAGNER, R. (1949), 'The employment interview: a critical summary', *Personn. Psychol.*, vol. 2, pp. 17–46.

WALSTER, E. (1966), 'Assignment of responsibility for an accident', *J. Person. soc. Psychol.*, vol. 3, pp. 73–9.

WARR, P. B., and HAYCOCK, V. (1970), 'Scales for a British personality differential', *Brit. J. soc. clin. Psychol.*, vol. 9, pp. 328–37.

WARR, P. B., and KNAPPER, C. (1968), *The Perception of People and Events*, Wiley.

WEDECK, J. (1947), 'The relationship between personality and "psychological ability" ', *Brit. J. Psychol.*, vol. 37, pp. 133–51.

WEINGARTEN, E. M. (1949), 'A study of selective perception in clinical practice', *J. Person.*, vol. 17, pp. 369–406.

WIGGIN, N., HOFFMAN, P. J., and TABER, T. (1969), 'Types of judges and cue utilisation in judgements of intelligence', *J. Person. soc. Psychol.*, vol. 12, pp. 52–9,

WITRYOL, S. L., and KAESS, W. A. (1957), 'Sex differences in social memory tasks', *J. abnorm. soc. Psychol.*, vol. 54, pp. 343–6.

WOODWORTH, R. S. (1938), *Experimental Psychology*, Holt, Rinehart & Winston.

YONGE, K. A. (1956), 'The value of the interview: an orientation and pilot study', *J. appl. Psychol.*, vol. 40, pp. 25–31.

ZIMMER, H. (1955), 'The role of conflict and internalised demands in projection', *J. abnorm. soc. Psychol.*, vol. 50, pp. 52–9.

ZUBIN, J. (1967), 'Classification of the behaviour disorders', *Ann. Rev. Psychol.*, vol. 18, pp. 373–406.

Further Reading

M. ARGYLE, *The Psychology of Interpersonal Behaviour*, Penguin, 1967. A good exposition of the social skill model, and review of the literature on non-verbal communication.

V. B. CLINE, 'Interpersonal perception', *Progress in Experimental Personality Research*, vol. 2, 1964. An account of the difficulties involved in measuring accuracy, which describes, among other things, the Behaviour Postdiction Test.

E. C. MAYFIELD, 'The selection interview: a re-evaluation of published research', *Personnel Psychology*, vol. 17, 1964. As useful critical review.

T. R. SABIN, R. TAFT and J. E. BAILEY, *Clinical Inference and Cognitive Theory*, Holt, Rinehart & Winston, 1960. A good exposition of inference and intuition models.

R. TAFT, 'The good judge of others', *Psychological Bulletin*, vol. 52, 1955. A review of the literature on generality of ability to judge, and characteristics of good judges.

R. TAGIURI, 'Person perception', in G. Lindzey and E. Aronson (eds.), *Handbook of Social Psychology*, vol. 3, Addison-Wesley, 1969. A detailed survey of progress in the area over the last decade.

P. E. VERNON, *Personality Assessment*, Methuen, 1964. A useful short review of the whole area; also has good accounts of psychiatric diagnosis, and of personality measurement techniques, and a very good discussion of the concepts of reliability and validity.

P. E. VERNON and J. B. PARRY, *Personnel Selection in the British Armed Forces*, University of London Press, 1949. An interesting account of selection methods used on a very large scale in the Second World War.

P. B. WARR and C. KNAPPER, *The Perception of People and Events*, Wiley, 1948. Contains a good review of the Semantic Differential literature, and also of 'impression formation' studies.

J. ZUBIN, 'Classification of the behaviour disorders', *Annual Review of Psychology*, vol. 18, 1967. Summarizes evidence on the reliability and validity of psychiatric diagnosis.

Index